Anonymous

The Handbook to Monterey and Vicinity

Anonymous

The Handbook to Monterey and Vicinity

ISBN/EAN: 9783743686755

Printed in Europe, USA, Canada, Australia, Japan

Cover: Foto ©Andreas Hilbeck / pixelio.de

More available books at **www.hansebooks.com**

THE HAND BOOK OF

MONTEREY

AND VICINITY.

" In a mantle of old traditions,
In the rime of a vanished day,
The shrouded and silent City
Sits by her crescent Bay."

THE HAND BOOK

TO

MONTEREY AND VICINITY:

CONTAINING

A BRIEF RESUMÉ OF THE HISTORY OF MONTEREY SINCE ITS DISCOVERY ;

A GENERAL REVIEW OF THE RESOURCES AND PRODUCTS OF MONTEREY
AND THE COUNTY; DESCRIPTIVE SKETCHES OF THE TOWN,
AND THE POINTS OF INTEREST IN THE NEIGHBORHOOD;
CARMEL MISSION AND VALLEY ; PACIFIC GROVE
RETREAT; POINT CYPRESS, POINT PINOS
AND THE LIGHT HOUSE ; SALINAS,
CASTROVILLE, SAN JUAN,
SAN ANTONIO MISSION,

AND OTHER PLACES OF INTEREST IN THE COUNTY.

A COMPLETE GUIDE BOOK,

For Tourists, Campers and Visitors.

MONTEREY, 1875.

AUTHORITIES QUOTED.

Records of Mission of San Carlos.   Junipera Serra, Juan Crespi,
    and others.
United States Coast Survey.
Three Years in California.   Walter Colton.
Natural Wealth of California.   Cronise.
U. S. Agricultural Reports.
Smithsonian Institute Reports.
Unpublished Memoranda.   Dr. C. A. Canfield.
California Scrap Book.
Resources of Monterey County.
Resources of San Benito County.
Overland Monthly.
The Californian.
Monterey Republican.
Monterey Herald.
Santa Cruz Sentinel.
Salinas City Index.
Salinas City Town Talk.
Castroville Argus.
San Francisco Alta, Call, Chronicle, and Examiner.

CONTENTS.

	PAGE.
Monterey, Poem, by E. E. Curtis	5
Historical Sketch	6
Portala's Cross, by Bret Harte	17
Monterey and Vicinity	19
Carmel Valley and Mission	25
Point Cypress	36
Monterey, Poem, by D. O'Connell	42
The Whale Fishery	44
Chinese Colony	49
Pacific Grove Retreat	50
Light House	54
Monterey, Poem, by Mrs. Annie E. Merritt	55
Monterey as a Port	57
The M. & S. V. R. R	60
Health and Climate, with Tables	63
Increase of Business	71
Town Officers, etc	72
Objects of Historical Interest	74
Our Pioneer Residents	82
Disinterested Opinions	83
Sea Bathing	85
Iron Springs	87

4 CONTENTS.

PAGE.

Coal Mines............................... 89
Our Wild Flowers......................... 89
Trades Directory 91
The County............................... 97
Salinas City...................... 111
Castroville 116
Moss Landing............................. 120
Santa Rita............................... 120
Soledad.................................. 120
Chualar 121
Gonzales................................. 121
Natividad.... 121
Soledad Mission.......................... 122
San Antonio Mission 123
San Juan Mission......................... 124
Hollister................................ 125
San Juan Township....................... 126
Advertisements..... 128

MONTEREY.

Like a maiden musing sadly o'er her suitors turned away,
Long she sat in lonely beauty close beside her crescent bay.

Heeding not the world of action that beyond her portals lay ;
Careless of the strife of nations, living only for to-day.

Dreaming of a golden future, while the present drifted by,
As a ship becalmed may linger 'neath the storm-cloud in the sky.

All her passions wrapped in slumber ; slowly through her languid veins
Flowed her blood, as in midsummer creeps the stream across the plains.

Never lover came to woo her, never woke she from her trance,
Like the mystic Sleeping Beauty in the pages of romance.

Till the fairy Prince of Progress smiled upon her hidden charms,
On her ripe lips quickly kissed her, reached and drew her to his arms.

At his touch she slowly started : Indolence her limbs had bound
While she lingered, idly dreaming, where the tasseled tree-tops sound ;

And though heart and soul were eager to accept the proffered love,
'Neath the tyrant's chain they struggled, as the wings of prisoned dove.

Not in vain she strives to free them ; for, behold ! the chain is burst !
Aided by the arm of Progress soon the last shall be the first.

Soon a queen among the cities that adorn our golden coast
Shall she stand, and in her glory, of her noble lover boast.

EDWIN EMMET CURTIS.

MONTEREY, July, 1875.

Historical Sketch of Monterey.

So intimately is the history of Monterey connected and inter-woven with that of California, and in a lesser degree, with that of Mexico and Spain, that to detail it faithfully and accurately would require more space than we have at our command. We propose, therefore, to sketch as briefly as possible some of the leading events of its history, from the period of its discovery until the present day.

Early in the spring of 1602, the Viceroy of Mexico, acting under instructions from Philip III of Spain, who was anxious to obtain possession of California, dispatched Don Sebastian Viscaiño, in com-mand of three small vessels, on a voyage of discovery up the coast. Their passage was rendered extremely slow by prevailing head winds, and the exploration of the peninsula, now known as Lower California, was not completed until the beginning of November. On the 10th of that month they arrived at the harbor of San Diego, where they remained ten days, and departed highly pleased with the climate, soil, and peaceful disposition of the Indians. After landing on Santa Catalina Island, and at other places, for the pur-pose of celebrating Mass, they rounded the Point of Pines, and cast anchor in the storm-sheltered waters of our beautiful bay on the 10th day of December, 1602.

Viscaiño, who was probably the first white man to place foot upon he soil of this town, took possession of the country in the name of the King of Spain. The holy sacrament was then partaken of under the spreading branches of an oak tree, at the mouth of a small ravine, and the spot named Monterey, in honor of Gaspar de Zuniga, Count de Monterey, the Viceroy of Mexico, who had fitted out the expedition.

Viscaiño was unprepared to establish a Mission; so, after a stay of eighteen days, he continued on his voyage; first however taking a full description of the country, its productions, and the character of the natives. He described the country as being clad in the deepest verdure, the soil most productive, the natives extremely docile, and, therefore easily converted. Although Viscaiño hoped soon to return with material for the founding of a Mission, his hopes were never realized, and Monterey still remained a wilderness.

Over 166 years elapsed ere Monterey was again visited by the white man. On July 14, 1769, Gaspar de Portala, Governor of Lower California, at the head of a party of sixty-five persons, set out from San Diego to rediscover Monterey. He arrived at Monterey, but failing to identify the place, merely erected a cross and proceeded on his way north.

The third attempt to establish a settlement at Monterey, however, proved more successful. The following extract from a letter of the leader of the expedition to Father Francisco Palou, gives a graphic account of the ceremonies attending the formal founding of the Mission of San Carlos de Monterey, by Padre Junipero Serra, on that memorable day, June 3rd, 1770.

" On the 31st of May, 1770, by favor of God, after rather a painful voyage of a month and a half, the packet *San Antonio*, commanded by Don Juan Perez, arrived and anchored in this beautiful port of Monterey, which is unadulterated in any degree from what it was when visited by the expedition of Don Sebastian Viscaiño, in 1602. It gave me great consolation to find that the land expedition had arrived eight days before us, and that Father Crespi and all others were in good health. On the third of June, being the holy day of Pentecost, the whole of the officers of sea and land, and all the people, assembled on a bank at the foot of an oak, where we caused an altar to be erected, and the bells rang; we then chanted the *Veni Creator*, blessed the water, erected and blessed a grand cross, hoisted the royal standard, and chanted the first mass that was ever performed in this place; we afterwards sung the *Salve* to Our Lady before an image of the illustrious Virgin, which occupied the altar; and at the same time preached a sermon, concluding the whole with a *Te Deum*. After this the officers took possession of the country in the name of the King, (Charles III) our Lord, whom God preserve. We then all dined together in a shady place on the beach; the whole ceremony being accompanied by many vollies and salutes by the troops and vessels."

Later, on the same day, was solemnized the first funeral, being that of a caulker named Alejo Nino, who died on board the *San Antonio* a few days previous. He was buried with the honors of the Church at the foot of the cross they had erected.

. The *San Antonio* soon sailed for Mexico, leaving behind Father Junipero, five priests, Lieutenant Pedro Fages and thirty soldiers. The Indians, as Viscaiño had predicted, were ready converts, and " seated under those dark Monterey pines, told ghostly stories of how brightly the crosses shone that each white man wore on his breast the first time they had passed through there, not knowing the place; and of the great cross that was planted by Portala before he knew he was at the spot he coveted; how it would grow at night till its point rested among the stars, glistening the while with a splendor that outshone the sun; that when their superstitious dread wore off they had approached, planted arrows and feathers in the earth around it, and hung strings of sardines, as their choicest offering, upon its arms." *

Monterey was at once selected as the capital of Alta California, and Portala appointed as its first governor. Owing to the small amount of available agricultural land within the semicircle of hills surrounding Monterey, the Mission was soon removed to the neighboring valley of Carmelo.† The presidio or military establishment, however, still remained at Monterey. This consisted of an enclosure about 300 yards square, containing a chapel, storehouses, offices, residences and barracks for the soldiers. It was located where the Catholic church now stands. A rude fort was built on the hill overlooking the bay, and armed with a few small cannon. These constituted the nucleus of the future town.

Calmly the years drifted away, scarcely causing a ripple upon the slowly swelling tide of progress. Governor succeeded governor, and each was content to render tribute to the Viceroy of Mexico, while the fruitful land over which he ruled maintained him in luxurious idleness. In 1822, Mexico, becoming tired of Spanish rule,

* Tuthill's History of California.
† A more complete account of the Mission is given in another chapter.
2

established herself as a separate empire. Upon receiving intelligence of this important event, Governor Pablo Vicente de Sola summoned a council of the principal military officials and church dignitaries at Monterey, and formally announced the action of their mother country. The council unanimously decided that henceforth California was subject to Mexico alone. The oaths were changed and Sola became the first Mexican governor, or more correctly, "Political Chief of the Territory." The apathetic inhabitants offered no resistance, and the change was effected without a struggle.

In 1828 the Mexican Congress adopted a plan of colonization, which authorized the Governors of dependent territories to grant unoccupied lands to all persons who properly petitioned for them, and agreed to cultivate and reside upon them a certain portion of the time. These grants were subject to the approval of the territorial legislature. Many of the old settlers availed themselves of the privilege thus accorded them and obtained a title to vast ranchos, then of little value, but destined in after years to render those who were fortunate enough to hold them immensely wealthy.

The harbor of Monterey was visited about this time by numerous vessels, which realized an enormous profit by trading their assorted cargoes for hides.

On the 25th of September, 1834, Hijar, Director of Colonization, arrived at Monterey on the brig *Natalia*, for the purpose of secularizing the Missions. The *Natalia*, which was the same vessel in which Napoleon the Great made his memorable escape from Elba, was thrown upon the beach by a storm and totally wrecked.

The remaining timbers of this historical vessel may yet be seen at low tide, a few yards east of the railroad wharf. The seculariza- tion scheme was successfully accomplished, and the missions placed under the charge of Governor Figueroa.

Figueroa, who was the best-ruler California had yet seen, died on the 29th of September, 1835. Then ensued a series of insurrections which were only terminated by the American conquest. A dissen- sion first arose between Nicholas Gutierrez, who was Governor after Figueroa's death, and Juan Bautista Alvarado, Secretary of the Territorial Deputation, concerning a question of Custom House discipline. Alvarado, who was a native Californian of talent and education, insisted so strongly upon his position that Gutierrez ordered his arrest. Before the warrant could be served Alvarado had escaped, and found refuge in the cabin of Isaac Graham, a pioneer of Santa Cruz. Here a plan was laid to seize Monterey and declare the independence of California. They organized a company of one hundred natives under Jose Castro, and fifty rifle- men led by Graham; entered Monterey at night; imprisoned the Governor and his soldiers in the presidio; and after firing one shot from a four-pounder, obtained possession of the town. Alvarado was declared Governor, and Guadalupe Vallejo placed at the head of the military.

Early in 1840, Governor Alvarado, who had become exceedingly jealous of all foreigners, especially of his former friend Graham, pre- tended to have received information of a deep-laid plot to overturn the government. Castro was ordered to arrest all connected with the conspiracy, and by a strategic movement succeeded in surprising and arresting nearly a hundred persons, principally Americans. Afterward, about twenty of the supposed ringleaders were transported in chains to San Blas. In July of the same year, the American man-of-war *St. Louis* and a French ship arrived at Monterey for the purpose of demanding satisfaction. Alvarado was so badly frightened at their arrival that he fled to the interior, on a pretext of business, and did not return to the Capital until the coast was again clear. For two years everything remained quiet.

In July, 1842, the foreigners, so summarily banished, unexpectedly returned on board a vessel furnished them by the Mexican Government, which had not approved of Alvarado's uncalled-for action. They brought the startling news that General Micheltorena had been appointed to both the civil and military command of California. He arrived at San Diego in August, and was traveling northward in grand style, when intelligence reached him that caused him to suddenly halt at Los Angeles. This was that Commander Jones, in command of the frigate *United States* and sloop-of-war *Cyane*, had taken possession of the country, and hoisted the Stars and Stripes at Monterey. Alvarado surrendered on the 20th of October, and California was, apparently, a portion of the American Union. The next day, however, Jones discovered that he had made a blunder—that Mexico was not yet at war with the United States—and therefore he gracefully hauled down the flag and apologized. Micheltorena now came to Monterey and assumed the duties of his office. He ruled until February 1st, 1845, when he was ousted by Vallejo, Alvarado and Castro, and Don Pio Pico placed in his stead.

The year 1846 was a notable one in the annals of Monterey. On July 7th, of that year, Commodore Sloat, who had arrived in the U. S. frigate *Savannah* a few days previously, dispatched Captain Mervine, at the head of 250 men, on shore, with instructions to hoist the American flag over Monterey. Amid the firing of cannon from the shipping in the harbor and the cheers of the assembled citizens, the glorious Stars and Stripes were raised, and a proclamation read, declaring California henceforth a portion of the United States. The people accepted the change with characteristic resignation, and Walter Colton was appointed the first Alcalde under the new regime.

Colton, who had previously been Chaplain of the frigate *Congress*, held the office of alcalde for three years, during which time he figured prominently in the affairs of the town. In connection with Semple, a pioneer from Kentucky, he established the first newspaper ever published in California. It was called the *Californian*, and made its first appearance on Saturday, August 15th, 1846. It was printed on paper originally intended for the manufacture of cigaritos, and was a little larger than a sheet of foolscap. The office was resurrected from the remains of a small concern formerly used for printing Roman Catholic tracts in Spanish. There being no W in the Spanish alphabet, they were compelled to use two V's (thus, VV) whenever a W occurred. The *Californian*, it is needless to say, was eagerly welcomed, and soon attained quite a circulation. It was finally merged into the *Alta California* when the latter paper was established at San Francisco.

The first jury summoned in California was empannelled by Col-

2*

ton, on September 4th, 1846.   It was composed of one-third Mexicans, one-third Californians, and the other third Americans.   This new system of trial proved eminently satisfactory, as it always must when properly administrated.   To Colton also belongs the honor of having erected the building, intended for a Town Hall and School House, which bears his name.

On the 29th of May, 1848, intelligence of the discovery of gold on the American Fork first reached Monterey.   The report was scarcely credited, yet it produced so much excitement that the Alcalde was induced to dispatch a special messenger to investigate its truth.   On the 12th of June he returned, bringing specimens of gold, and a story of its lavish abundance more marvelous than an Arabian Night's tale.   Then commenced the grand rush to the mines, which almost depopulated the town, and from which it has never fully recovered.

On the 3d of June, 1849, (the 79th anniversary of the settlement of Monterey) Governor Riley issued a " Proclamation recommending the formation of a State Constitution, or plan of a Territorial Government."   In pursuance of this proclamation, the Convention for forming a State Constitution met in Colton Hall (now used as a school house) on the first of the following September. Monterey was represented by the following delegates : H. W. Halleck, T. O. Larkin, C. T. Botts, P. Ord and L. Dent.

The labors of the Convention were successful beyond its most sanguine expectations.   A Constitution, remarkable for the wisdom and liberality of its provisions, was adopted, and shortly afterward ratified by the people.   Upon adjournment, a salute of thirty-one guns was fired, which echoed grandly back from the pine-wreathed hills, proclaiming that soon a queen would step forth among the sisterhood of States.

Although the convention accomplished such great results, it effectually blighted the fair prospects of Monterey by the passage of a resolution removing the state capital to San Jose.

By an Act of the Legislature, passed April 30th, 1851, the town was duly incorporated. Philip A. Roach, who was then Alcalde, was elected the first Mayor. His administration was unmarked by any events worthy of special mention. He was succeeded by Gilbert Murdock, of the firm of Curtis & Murdock, merchants, who was followed by W. H. McDowell.

Monterey did not long remain a city, for by an Act approved May 11th, 1853, her charter was amended and the control of municipal affairs vested in a board of three trustees.

In 1859 the town found herself so much in debt that it became necessary, in order to meet her obligations, to sell the greater portion of the Pueblo grant. Such extravagance brought the trustees into disrepute, and at the next session of the Legislature the charter was again amended in such a manner as to render their powers, either for good or for evil, exceedingly limited.

During the legislative session of 1869–70 an attempt at reincorporation was made ; the bill passed the Assembly, but was defeated in the Senate. Another attempt was then made, but in some manner the bill again miscarried. A third effort to obtain the desired result proved somewhat more successful. In 1873–74 the " Act to Re-incorporate the City of Monterey" was carried through both

Houses and reached the Governor, who, it is alleged, failed to return it within the specified time. Be this as it may, nothing more was heard of the bill, and Monterey still remained under the nominal control of its trustees. The board at present consists of S. B. Gordon, President; H. Escolle, Treasurer; and W. H. Bryan Clerk.

Simultaneously with the growth of Salinas City, which was becoming the liveliest town in the county, arose the question of county seat removal. Monterey had held this honor ever since the organization of the county, and the attempt of her younger rival to wrest it from her was bitterly opposed. In spite of her efforts, however, a petition signed by the requisite number of voters was presented to the Board of Supervisors, who, as in duty bound, ordered an election; this was held on the 6th of November, 1872, the day of the presidential election. The result was a victory for Salinas City, and on the following February the county seat was removed to its present location.

From that time until the commencement of the narrow gauge railroad in April, 1874, the fortunes of Monterey were at their lowest ebb. Business of every description was almost stagnant; enterprise and improvement seemed to have no foothold within her quiet precincts, and aptly was she called " The sleepy hollow of California." Like Atri in Abbruzo, described by Longfellow as

> " One of those little places that have run
> Half up the hill beneath a blazing sun,
> And then sat down to rest, as if to say,
> 'I climb no farther upward, come what may,' "

She rested in peaceful somnolence—a veritable land of lotus eaters—where the struggles of the outside world found no abiding place.

The completion of the railroad marked a new era in the history of Monterey. Connected with the fertile Salinas Valley, having a safe and commodious harbor, together with ample shipping facilities, there is no fear of a relapse into her former state of lethargy. Although no great improvements have as yet been accomplished, every day brings increased prosperity, and slowly but surely Monterey is advancing to take her destined place among the cities of the coast.

PORTALA'S CROSS.*

BY BRET HARTE.

Pious Portala, journeying by land,
Reared high a cross upon the heathen strand,
    Then far away
Dragged his slow caravan to Monterey.

The mountains whispered to the valleys, " good !"
The sun, slow sinking in the western flood,
    Baptized in blood
The holy standard of the Brotherhood.

*See " Historical Sketch " for the incident referred to in this poem.

The timid fog crept in across the sea,
Drew near, embraced it, and streamed far and free,
        Saying :   " O ye
Gentiles and Heathen, this is truly He."

All this the Heathen saw ; and when once more
The holy Fathers touched the lonely shore—
        Then covered o'er
With shells and gifts—the cross their witness bore.

MONTEREY AND VICINITY.

Monterey has undoubtedly all the natural advantages for becoming one of the leading watering places and summer resorts of
the State. Her natural beauty of scenery, the crescent-shaped,
pine-fringed hills, sloping down through park-like groves and
flowery swards on to the quaint old Spanish town nestling at their
feet, and on again to the silvery sands and creamy ripple of the
surf of the broad, beautiful, blue waters of the bay; the eye at
length resting on the bold outlines of the lofty Santa Cruz mountains, towering to the sky. On the right we have Fremont's Peak
and the Gabilan Range, breaking the long view over the rolling
plains. The light and shadows create a perpetual change, and the
variety of scenes is such that the eye never tires of gazing at nature's handiwork. Our sands are without rival—one long, bold
sweep of wide, gently sloping, clean white sands—the perfection of
a bathing beach. Around from the old wharf to the light-house
there are nooks and alcoves such as the poets love to sing as
the haunts of the mermaids. The great desideratum of a seaside resort is a beach upon which children can with safety play and
bathe, and such we certainly have. Sea mosses, shells, and pebbles
we have in great variety, while for the amateur naturalist, geologist, mineralogist, and several scientists, there are unrivaled oppor-

[19]

tunities for augmenting their information and collections. Tire of the town, and you can have a trip to Carmel or Pescadero Bays, beautiful in the extreme; the old Mission of Carmel, full of historical interest and beauty; Point Cypress, or the light-house on Point Pinos; the Hot Springs at Tassajara, or go fishing either in the bay or the rivers of the neighbouring mountains as they flow through the rocky cañons; if of a nautical turn of mind you can have sailing or rowing in safe waters. The salubrity of the climate is almost proverbial. Let a worn-out invalid, or a man whose brains have been racked with toil, come to us—the magnetic influence of the atmosphere grants him sleep and restful health.

From our point of view, also, Monterey has great industrial resources in addition to her claims as a pleasant location and fine climate, but these resources are in embryo, and await the hand of energy and capital to bring them to the birth. Communication with the outside world was the first great desideratum, and that, within the past twelve months, has been to a great extent accomplished; the narrow-gauge railroad to Salinas connects us by land with San Francisco, the Salinas Valley, and indirectly with all points of the State. By sea we have regular and frequent intercourse with the city and the ports of the coast. The proposed extension of the railroad to Hollister and a loop-line to Castroville will be the means of bringing to Monterey for direct shipment to foreign ports the greater portion of the grain and other products of the fertile counties of Monterey and San Benito. It is also proposed, we believe, to connect the M. & S. V. R. R., via Soledad, with Santa Barbara in one direction; and in the other with the Watsonville and Santa Cruz Railroad.

These communications not only offer a means of carrying away the products when made, but indirectly create a demand for them by assisting in the subdivision of large ranches into small farms, and the consequent settling-up of the country and the increased wealth of its inhabitants, the production of the raw article and the demand for its manufacture. The industrial contributions to this demand which Monterey could make had she the men of enterprise and capital to carry them out, are the following, amongst others : Tanneries—the stock-raisers of the county can supply the hides, and the materials for tanning we have at hand cheaper than in most parts of the State ; the same remarks apply to wool and cloth mills, and shoe factories. San Francisco has had to send to the East for bricks, while we have the clay capable of making bricks of very good quality, as is shown by those already turned out ; the pottery clay is good, and ware is already manufactured in small quantities. Our sand is considered the best in the State for glass-making, and is exported in large quantities to San Francisco for that purpose. San Jose is making building-blocks out of the sands of the Coyote—our sands are of purer quality, and as superior to theirs for that purpose as it is possible to imagine. Experts say that our indications of coal and iron are of the most promising character, and no less than six or seven companies are vigorously prospecting in this direction. Many other minerals are also found in small quantities, but have not yet been thoroughly searched for. Lime kilns, flour mills and planing mills are wanted, and there are good openings for them. Stock-raising, farming, and dairying are sure roads to fortune in this county, and there are yet openings for

3

all.   Our fisheries, whale, and edible fish, are increasing in importance.   The great State Camp-meeting location at Pacific Grove,
close to town, will give ample opportunities for strangers to invest
in small residential properties, and more than one land-owner has
announced his intention of dividing his land into building lots this
year.

Such are the views of some of our resources, but above all we
have that priceless boon of heaven, a healthy climate ; no agues
and fever, no chills or rheumatism, no sickness save that of old
age.   The class of men who will be welcomed here are men of
energy and capital.   As regards our town of Monterey, we have
enough grocers, saloonists, and mechanics ; what is actually needed
is a first-class hotel, or manufactories—above all, men who will stay
with us a year or two and help to build us up, and not fly away
with the first breeze of disappointment.

We require two first-class hotels, competent to accommodate
visitors by the hundreds and not by the score—one in the town
and one on the hill-side, or at Littletown—there are two sites
admirably adapted for the purpose, which will be donated free of
expense to any one erecting the buildings ; a race course, which
might be advantageously placed in Toombs' grove, or at the foot of
the Carmel road ; bathing houses along the beach, and one good
large *etablissement de bains*, after the French fashion, in which
one can take his hot or cold bath, and afterwards find amusement
for the body and mind, or lounge away the day luxuriously and
idly.   Handsome stores and a thriving town would soon follow as a
matter of course.   It is no idle dream of a sanguine visionary to

believe that all these things will come sooner or later, and that Monterey *will* become one of the most fashionable summer resorts for the wealthy. Santa Cruz, Aptos, and Santa Barbara have already become so. Their natural advantages are, in many respects, inferior to those possessed by Monterey ; but they have that which Monterey has not—American enterprise, and capital to assist it; a hospitable welcome to the stranger, and the hand of friendship extended to all who will cast in their lot with them.

Monterey dreams idly on, and will so dream until a fresh race of men, such men as are now building up our California cities, enters her dreamy Eden, and, with the rough but kindly hand of energy, arouses her from her lethargy.

It cannot be long before this change takes place. All down the coast, towns, not so well favored as Monterey, are being built up, and her turn *must* come. San Francisco is now too firmly fixed to fear the competition of Monterey, and that opposition on the part of the press to her advancement, which has done so much to keep our town back, will now probably be withdrawn, if we may judge from the spirit of fair play exhibited by the *Alta*, *Chronicle*, and *Call*, in admitting in their columns lengthy letters from Monterey.

One very natural thought must arise in the minds of reflective readers—and it is to such that we address this work—and it is this : If Monterey is so blessed by Nature as you state it to be, how is it that she is so decayed in her glory and sunk in her worth ? How is it, that, while San Francisco, Santa Cruz, San Luis, Santa Barbara, and many other towns, have sprung from nothingness into position and wealth, Monterey has only retrograded from wealth and position into comparative oblivion ?

To such a thought we would reply : The gold fever caused a migration of the people from Monterey ; the establishment of Sacramento and San Francisco, whither congregated all the energy and enterprise, and the consequent removal of the capital to a more populated spot; the want of communication with the interior farming country, Monterey not having in her immediate vicinity resources or population sufficient to support herself by herself; and, lastly, the character of her inhabitants—good-tempered, kind and hospitable, easy-going and listless, as are all the Spanish-speaking races—they lived to enjoy life easily and comfortably, not to be harassed with the cares and turmoils attending energy and enterprise. Nature was bountiful to them, and they lived on Nature's gifts. Mirth, music, and " mañana," with just sufficient exertion as was absolutely requisite to provide for their necessities, constituted their rule of life. They drifted down with the stream. The capital went, and then the county seat—and no great exertion was made to retain either of them. A few men looked ahead, and worked, and they are now enjoying their reward ; but the majority adopted the *dolce far niente* habits of the natives, and did nothing but exist.

There is also another section of residents, whose policy it has been to retard, by every means in their power, the growth of the place, and consequent entry of competition, to be soon followed, as they truly thought, by the loss of their influence, prosperity, and position ; fortunately, in the ordinary course of nature their retirement to more congenial realms cannot be far distant.

Disquieting and prejudicial rumors of bad land titles have also been sown broadcast, by interested parties, to prevent the sales of property to willing investors.

The railroad has changed the state of affairs not a little ; and events of the past year clearly prove, that, with an American population working in harmony with the more enlightened portion of the old residents and natives, a great and prosperous city may yet be built upon the site of the old capital.   It is for our readers to pay us a visit and judge for themselves of our prospects.

Carmel Mission and Valley.

The Valley of the Carmello River affords attractions to lovers of Nature such as few other places in the State can furnish.   The passing traveler — be he artist or antiquary, geologist or " grizzly shootist," piscator or pedestrian, " prospector" or pleasure seeker—may here find something congenial to his taste.   The road from Monterey passes the old Cuartel, and branches off to the right, having on one side a woody ravine and low, flat, level lands, studded, park-like, with live oaks ; on the other, the well-wooded, pine-feathered hills.   Half way up the steep hill, we command a mag-

3*

nificent view of Monterey, Santa Cruz, and the Castroville and
Salinas Valleys, with Fremont Peak and the Gabilan for a background. Reaching the summit, and looking to the right, through
a pretty wooded glen, the eye rests upon the broad ocean. A
shady road, up hill and down dale, with ever-changing views, all
beautiful, until the hill overlooking the Carmel vale is reached,
and therê we have a sight worthy of Eden in its happiest days.
On our right, the mountain, which looms before us, heavy and
massive, gloomy and severe, tapers off into a narrow, pine-fringed,
sea-girt point, against which the blue waters of the Carmel Bay
dash with ever varying beauty. This point is named Point Lobos,
so called from the " lobos del mar " (sea wolves, a species of seal)
that collect on the point, and can be seen from the shore in large
numbers. Silvery sands line the Bay, whiter almost than the sea
foam as it splashes and sprays against the dark green background.
To our right, the valley winds between the mountains, and at our
feet the Carmel glistens in the sunlight as it flows through the
willows to the sea. Descend the hill, turn to the right, and we
have reached the ruins of the old Mission. Hardly a pleasing
sight to any one possessing the bump of veneration even in the
smallest degree. ‚ A few ruined, broken-down adobes encircle a
dreary, desolate, semi-roofless building, beautiful even in decay—all
that is left of the second Mission in California, and one that in its
day must have been a grand edifice, for it bears unmistakable
evidence of an accurate knowledge of architecture, blended with a
bold conception in its detail and skillful workmanship, considering
the materials at hand. In 1770, a little more than one hundred

years ago, the venerable Franciscan, Junipero Serra, wandering over mountains and through vales, preaching the gospel of good tidings and great joy, hung his bells on a tree in this spot, and houted, " " Hear, hear, O ye gentiles, come to the Holy Church !" and thus gathered around him the Indian tribes of the Rumsienes or Runsiens, the Escelenes or Eslens, the Eclemaches and Achastlies. Captivated by the scenery, its proximity to the sea, and, above all, the beautiful stream of water and the general fertility of the valley, Serra

> "Sought in these mountain solitudes a home;
> He founded here his convent, and his rule
> Of prayer and work, and counted work as prayer."

He labored zealously among his native converts, and died in 1784, loved by them all. He lies buried in the Mission which he founded.

Visitors should inspect the curious old pictures and relics of antiquity in the chapel on the right.

We climb up into the deserted belfry, where erst the bells have pealed, calling the worshipers to mass; and rouse from his day-dreams its sole tenant—the traditional old, grey owl, that stares wonderingly at us from its saucer-like eyes.

As we sit upon one of the fallen roof-beams, and gaze upon the shattered font, the broken-down crosses, the ruined altar, and the general scene of devastation and desolation around us, and remember that this is one of the most ancient and important historical monuments of California, the home and the grave of the moral hero of the age, the true pioneer of California progress—Junipero Serra, and the tomb of no less than fifteen Governors of this State, a

painful feeling controls us.   Carmel Mission is the old Westminster
Abbey of the State, the mausoleum of the great and the good, and
the nation rewards the services of the past by giving up
the dust of the good and brave to the guardianship of
gophers and squirrels.   Thorns and briars, nettles and loathsome
weeds, adorn their graves.   A few short years, and naught will remain of. this holy edifice save an undistinguishable mass of debris.
A few more years, and it will be too late—even now it will be somewhat difficult—to restore it.   Whatever is done should be done
quickly, nobly, and generously, for the present state of the Mission
is a standing reproach to the church which owns it and a disgrace
to the whole State of California.   It is a monument for the preser-
vation of which every Californian, especially the wealthy Pioneers,
should exert themselves to have the work of renovating the building commenced as soon as possible.   The day will come when history will mark with contempt the present generation for permitting
the decay of this, the last resting place of the great and good
Padre Junipero.

On the 4th of November of each year the Monterey Padre holds
a religious festival in honor of San Carlos, the patron saint of Carmello.   The ruins are decorated with flowers and evergreens, and
mirth and festivity are the order of the day.

In the Mission soil were raised the first potatoes cultivated in California.   In 1771, an inventory of stock showed the Mission to be possessed of 19 head of cattle, 10 mules, and 4 horses.   The height
of its prosperity was reached in 1825.   It then owned 87,600 head
of cattle, 60,000 sheep, 2,300 calves, 1,800 horses, 365 yoke of

oxen, a large amount of merchandise, and $40,000 in specie. There is a tradition among the natives, that this money was buried somewhere, on the report that a vessel, supposed to be a pirate, had been seen off the coast.

Passing down the coast road the geologist may pursue his investigations; or by obtaining a "permit" from Mr. A. Manuel, the obliging secretary of the "Monterey Coal Mine Company," may visit that mine and judge for himself of the prospects of our coal deposits.

Still further down the coast, he may find more coal mines, wild and romantic scenery, grizzly bears, deer, trout-fishing, and other interesting and exciting "kill-times."

Returning, he will find a small and pretty bay, forming a splendid fishing boat harbor, and occupied by a company of Portuguese whalers and Chinese fishermen.   Here fresh fish and salmon-spearing may be had.

Returning to the valley, we pass on the hill-side a substantial modern building, Mr. Gregg's house.   His ranch is notable on account of more than one fortunate owner having made a comfortable "pile" on potatoes, the quantity and quality of which are very good.

Journeying up the Carmel valley and passing the second dairy farm on the Haight Ranch, (Mr. McDonald's) he will see to his right, across the river, the mouth of a cañon, to the left of which a number of small shanties constitute the "rancheria."   In one of these shanties there lately died an Indian woman who was a "muchacha" of some twenty-five summers when the Mission was formed.

The road passing up the cañon leads to the Potrero and San Francisquito ranchos, belonging to ,the Sargent Bros., and one of the residences of B. W. Sargent, a gentleman deservedly popular throughout the county; also to the bee and fruit ranch of Messrs. Smith & Wright, whose red-cheeked peaches and luscious grapes are justly celebrated. There is also a quicksilver mine in their neighborhood.

Continuing our journey along the main Carmel road, we come to the James Meadows grant. Mr. Meadows is one of the oldest of the Pioneers, he having come to Monterey in 1837. The school-house is upon this gentleman's land.

The next farm is held by Mr. Berwick, an English gentleman, whose enterprising experiments in agriculture cannot fail to be pro-ductive of great benefit to the State, and let us heartily wish it, to himself.

The dairy of the Snively Bros. is the next farm. ·Their butter commands the same price in the San Francisco markets as any of the first-class fancy dairies, and upon more than one occasion the· price has been higher.

They planted, four years ago, as an experiment, two almond ·trees, two years old. One of them is now twenty feet high, with a spread of twenty feet, and a girth, one foot from the ground, of three feet. The tree bears a good quality of fruit. Their vines are healthy. There is one little fellow about eighteen inches high, which has four large bunches of grapes upon it. The peach, apri-cot, pear, and nectarine trees are simply loaded with fruit. Cher-ries and strawberries thrive well.

Their orange trees have not had a fair trial at present, but pomegranates thrive well.

The ranch of Thomas Bralee is next reached. He came to Monterey first in 1844, returning to reside in 1847. The landscape here is very beautiful—hanging rocks and craggy buttresses.

The Laurelles ranch adjoins Mr. Bralee's, is one and one-half leagues in extent, and is the property of Spaulding & Co. Mr. S. is the well known professor of circular saw dentistry in San Francisco, and is here engaged in the laudable endeavour to make a somewhat wild tract of country " blossom as the rose." The road runs through very romantic and picturesque scenery, and the traveler may readily recognize the glossy green fragrant foliage of the laurel trees (*Oreodaphne Californica*) from which the ranch derives its name.

There is some good trout-fishing in the mountain streams, south of the Carmelo River, on the Government land abutting on this and the next ranch.

Los Tularcitos, of five and one-fourth leagues in extent, is the property of A. J. Ougheltree, a pioneer of '49. This fine tract of land situate in Europe might well constitute a ducal domain. In California, however, it merely passes as a " fine ranch."

The first house passed on the road is in what is known as the Chupinos Cañon, and is occupied by a dairyman; the next is Mr. O.'s dwelling house, charmingly situated near a small lagoon of spring water. Presuming our geologist to be also a palæontologist, he may, by inquiring of Mr. O., have an opportunity of examining some mammoth palæontological remains that are visible hereabouts.

Leaving the main road, and striking over the hills, south of Mr. O.'s house, the Jachagua Valley is reached. Retracing your steps to Mr. O.'s house, and again pursuing the main road, we pass S. P. Gordon's ranch, Los Conejos, three-fourths league ; Government land succeeds to this, occupied by Messrs. Finch, Robinson, James, and others. Near Mr. James' house the wagon road ends, and some ten miles of trail leads to the last glory of Carmel,

The Tassajara Hot Springs,

About forty-five miles from Monterey. There are here some dozen hot mineral springs—reported to be very effective remedial agents. " All the ills that flesh is heir to," barring consumption, may here find alleviation or cure. The late Dr. C. A. Canfield, our Monterey savant, forwarded some of the water to the Smithsonian Institute, to be analyzed ; and it was reported the richest spring then known in the United States. Thirty-two distinct ingredients were found therein. The water reaches the surface of the earth at 140 to 150 degrees Fahrenheit. Mr. John Borden, the present proprietor, reports some remarkable cures.

The proprietor is endeavoring to form a joint stock company to build a comfortable hotel and bath houses. Visitors can be accommodated either with " al fresco " lodgings, in which case they should carry their own necessaries, save provisions of all kinds, which can be furnished to them; or board and lodging can be found for a limited number.

Having completed his course of baths, our traveler may now proceed to the Mission of Soledad, twenty-five miles hence, or to the Mission of San Antonio, through the Reliz Cañon, about the same distance.

Throughout the whole of Carmel the hunter may find sport in plenty. Quails, rabbits, and hares are abundant, only too abundant for the farmer's good. Deer are to be found in the hills, and bear are in force towards the coast.

The products of the Valley are beef, butter, cheese, potatoes, and pork. Early potatoes are raised on the coast, and last season Mr. Gregg shipped 6,000 sacks of late potatoes that were noted in the market for their superior quality.

Whale oil and dried fish are also produced to a great extent.

For salubrity of climate, Carmel may fairly be considered unexcelled, possibly unsurpassable in the world.

Crops rarely fail on well tilled land, and even in years of drouth, grasses do not entirely forget to grow.

The following letter, on the coast lands of this county, we copy from the Santa Clara *Echo :*

" EDITORS ECHO :—Thinking a short communication in regard to this county might be acceptable, I send you the following account of its advantages as a district wherein settlers may procure desirable farming and grazing lands.

" There is a section of country south of here, (Monterey) lying directly on the coast—principally Government land—many valuable

4

portions of which are still unoccupied, that for climate, soil, and general adaptability for grazing purposes, cannot be excelled in the United States, which is saying a great deal. There is a steep range of mountains, running on a line with the ocean, and not far from it. On the slope of this range, facing the ocean, there is some of the finest land you ever gazed upon, comprising tables, or ridges, and pretty little valleys. In the deep gulches intervening there is the greatest abundance of the finest redwood and tan-bark oak; and in almost every one of these gulches there is a running stream of water the year round, while one or two approach almost the proportions of rivers. The grass continues fresh and green the entire year. When stock is once driven into this range there is no danger of their straying out; indeed, you may stand in your doorway and see them easily during the whole day. To add to the many other advantages that this beautiful section of country possesses over other parts of the State, is the fact that there is but one Spanish grant between the Carmello and San Luis Obispo, a distance of from eighty to one hundred miles.

" It is a paradise for hunters, or for those who desire to live cheap and do but little work; yet it might not be deemed such by one who owned a fine place on the line of your Alameda, but we are not all so fortunate as to be possessed of such valuable property. Deer, quail, and rabbits abound in abundance, while in the larger streams trout are plenty; then, if you dislike this sport, you can go down to the ledges in front of your little cot, and fish in the surf for rock-cod, which are very plenty, and easily caught. But the principal feature is its remarkable climate, it being entirely free from frost throughout the year—at least, none near the ocean, although on the hills it may be cold enough. To assure you further, I will give you a little of my personal experience. During Christmas week I was down the coast, some ten miles from here, (Monterey) prospecting for coal, (and here let me inform you that fine prospects of gold, silver, coal, and other minerals have been found in this section) and while camping with some Spaniards, on their "squat,". I soon felt the remarkable difference in the climate there and that of other sections north, although we were only a short distance from them. At night I slept on the mud floor of the barn, with only a little hay under me, with a thin blanket and a quilt for covering; and although the wind blew pretty fresh from the ocean, and you could put your hand anywhere through the crevices in the shakes that covered the barn, I had to throw off the quilt during the night, it being uncomfortably warm. In the morning before sunrise I could work quite comfortably without coat or vest; yet it is never hot or sultry during the summer season.

"On that night, as I learned afterwards, pumps and water-pipes froze in other places. After breakfast, while we were walking through a field, one of the Spaniards called my attention to some weeds under our feet; and there, exposed to my view, lay the tenderest plant that grows in California, it being no less than the Chile pepper, and that, too, in full bloom. 'How is that for high,' on a New Year's day? He also pulled up a potato vine, with a new potato hanging to it that was as large as a common sized hen egg.

"You will doubtless ask why such a country should remain

unsettled to this late day in California. I answer as best I can. There is, as yet, but a very sparse population, and the country in question has been almost inaccessible till within a few years, mainly on account of the bad roads, or rather, the entire lack of them. Up to some three years ago there was little more than a horse trail below the Carmello ; but now you can go with a wagon for about six miles from that stream. Below the present terminus, I am told that the country looks splendid, and that the timber through that country is heavy and plenty. I have been informed that claims can be bought quite cheap, say from $300 to $1,000 ; or claims can be taken up. Although the gulches are steep and the bends in the road are sharp, you can haul with a good span of horses five or six hundred pounds. The population are all males ; I hear of only one woman being down there. You will bear in mind that new settlers do not always represent the best society.

" Yours,   C. S.

" MONTEREY, February 7th."

Cypress Point.

Cypress Point is the one spot more perfectly adapted than any other place in the State for picnics and camping out.

Start out along the Carmel road, and take the path through the woods ; climb the hill, and, resting on the flower-bedecked turf, surrounded by ferns and groves, take in the view. Adown the wooded slope, carpeted with a profusion of flowers of all colors under the sun, the brown, barren-looking moorlands of the Salinas plain rising and falling like an inanimate sea of motionless billows, with here and there a bright emerald patch of some small, well-tilled farm shining like a rough-set jewel. The stern and sombre ' Gabilan range, with its serrated ridges' and dark clusters of pine woods, mellowed down with a filmy haze enshrouding its base. On our left, the beautifully blue waters of the Bay of Monterey, as smooth as a lake, half crescented with the lofty Santa Cruz range, its pine-feathered ridges, the white sands upon which the milk-white foam creeps and crawls with a sinuous motion like some huge leviathan of the deep. The azure heavens flecked with clouds. The whole panorama is one which the all-souled artist lives and loves to paint. Surely the " NAPLES OF THE NEW WORLD " is the Bay of Monterey.

On once again. We now enter a well shaded road, and catch charming glimpses, here and there, of the grand old Carmel range, and then suddenly there bursts upon our entranced sight a panorama of sky, ocean, and woods. The broad Pacific is only distinguishable from the heavens above it, by its glittering sheen as the sunlight plays upon its heaving breast. Anon, a little snow-flake of foam dances on the molten surface as one billow, more playful than the rest, shakes its snowy crest, or the white sails of a ship appear, as swan-like she glides along the water. The weird forest, with its gaunt, ghoul-like, black pines, moaning in

4*

harmony with the ceaseless roar of the waves as the breeze plays through the branches. Cold and uninviting is the distant view of this grim protector of the mysterious shades of the melancholy cypress. Enter the forest, and as you pass through the flowery glades the fragrance of the shrubs and the songs of the birds fall pleasantly on the senses. Pass on, and crossing an open space of green turf, startling the rabbits and quail, we enter another grove; the sun-flecks through the moss-hung and bearded trees, creating a pleasant, subdued light, such as is met with in the ancient minsters and Moorish alcazars of Europe. An involuntary thrill of delight runs through one, and from the storehouse of the mind rushes a flood of memory of childhood's days with its ancient legends, of enchanted groves and fairies. A few steps further, and the mystical grove is reached and crossed, and we gaze with rapture on the beauty of the sea coast. Surely God's world, beautiful as it is, can scarcely show fairer spots.

Landward the imperturbable cypress grove, silent as the Pyramids, mystical as the Sphinx, the gnarled gray trunks supporting the golden green branches—a fit haunt for departed spirits, a Merlin, or a slumbering cot for a child of Cain.

> " *Cain.*   Cypress! 'tis a gloomy tree,
>   As if it mourned o'er what it shadows;
>   Wherefore didst thou choose it
>   For our child's canopy?
>   *Adah.*   Because its branches
>   Shut out the sun like night, and therefore seem'd
>   Fitting to shadow slumber.
>   *Cain.*   Ay, the last and longest."

The sierras of the Santa Lucia droop down into the sea, brown, barren, and velvety, like some old dust-begrimed tome in the old library at home, uninviting on the outside but containing untold riches under its gloomy and unforbidding garb.   The ill starred Moro rock lifts its dome-shaped head with threatening aspect, warning mariners of the dangers of a rock-bound coast.   The craggy rocks jut out into the ocean, and the playful breakers as they dash upon them send aloft showers of spray white as driven snow, while the sunlight shines through the bright green billows as they curl and dash along in their impetuous, never-ending race. At our feet the silvery crystal sands are sprinkled with glistening abelone shells, sea polished, and the varied colors of the beautiful sea mosses.   Little pools teem with marine life and form a perfect aquaria, and the broad Pacific sweeps on in its uncontrollable course, bearing upon its bosom the wealth of empires.

Cross the point through the woody glades towards Point Pinos, passing pretty bays with white crystal sands and shelving beaches. Here the billows charge in with a greater impetuosity, but well in hand they break in a creamy ripple at the foot of the green-patched sand dunes.   The black pines from which the point was named three hundred years ago, almost skirt the water.   The mountains of Santa Cruz bound the view.   The many-plumaged sea birds flit by, and the sea lions dive under the foaming billows.   Stay and watch the setting sun gild the trees and cast a golden haze upon the swelling waters, and then ride home through the moonlit groves, and if your trip to Cypress Point has not been a happy one blame yourself, for possibly you may have forgotten that

> "He who joy would win,
> Must share it—happiness was born a twin."

· The Monterey Cypress.

We extract the following from a letter written by the late Dr. Canfield to the "Monterey Republican:"

" Very few ornamental trees are so easily made to grow in this part of California, or are so useful when grown, as the Monterey Cypress. Some trees, it is true, are easier raised and grow faster, but are good for nothing when grown, and speedily decay. * *

" The Monterey Cypress, it is unnecessary for me to say to those who have seen it, is a beautiful evergreen, grows rapidly, is thick, stout, and graceful, attaining a height of 40 to 60 feet. The largest trunk I measured in the grove at Point Cypress, was nineteen feet and two inches in circumference at three feet above the ground ; or about six feet and four inches in diameter. The timber is very durable, and makes excellent posts and rails. The cones, or globules, are produced every year, and are about the size of a large filbert. The seed is, in shape and size, like onion seed, and may be sown in the same way and in the same sort of soil.

The cones do not fall from the trees, and the seed is retained in them at Cypress Point, where the trees are kept almost constantly damp by the fog that rolls in from the ocean, till it often becomes mouldy and worthless. * * * With good seed it is as easy to raise Cypress trees as it is to raise onions or parsnips. But great care must be taken in transplanting them from the seed bed in the nursery, not to let the roots dry. This should be done just so soon in the fall as the ground becomes thoroughly moist, and the more dirt taken up with the roots the better. As soon as the ground begins to get dry in the spring or summer, the trees should be well watered every two or three days, sufficiently to keep the ground around their roots moist. And the second year, also, if any of the trees look feeble or unthrifty, they should be well watered. If planted on dry land, they cannot be injured by plentiful watering. The danger is that they will not have enough.

" The botanical name of the Monterey cypress is *Cupressus Macrocarpa*, of Hartweg: it was afterwards called *C. Macrabiana* by a Scotch florist, Murray, but this latter name is not used among botanists. Besides the large cypress, we have a very interesting dwarf species growing on the barren hills near town, and in a few other localities along the Coast. The *Cupressus Goveniana*, Gordon. It is a miniature tree, never more than ten feet high, but often loaded with cones, or galbules, when a foot high. Some botanists have not been willing to admit that this is anything more than a variety of the *Macrocarpa*, but I have proved by careful observation, by cultivation, etc., that it is a good species, and that it comes true from the seed; and I believe there is no longer any doubt of its being a distinct species. This, although a dwarf, does not grow bushy or straggling, but upright, straight and tree-like, and with a thin or sparse foliage, making a very curious and pretty ornament for cultivation, with its thick clusters of cones. Like the large Monterey Cypress, it is easily raised from seed. * * * The Monterey Cypress, though naturally growing in a few very limited localities along the coast near Monterey, readily grows almost anywhere in this State by taking a little care and observing the before mentioned precautions."

MONTEREY.

BY DANIEL O'CONNELL.

In a mantle of old traditions,
In the rime of a vanished day,
The shrouded and silent city
Sits by her crescent bay.

The ruined fort on the hill-top,
Where never a bunting streams,
Looks down, a cannonless fortress,
On the solemn city of dreams.

Gardens of wonderful roses,
Climbing o'er roof, tree and wall,
Woodbine and crimson geranium,
Hollyhocks, purple and tall,

Mingle their odorous breathings
With the crisp, salt breeze, from the sands,
Where pebbles and sounding sea shells
Are gathered by children's hands.

Women with olive faces,
And the liquid southern eye,
Dark as the forest berries
That grace the woods in July,

Tenderly train the roses,
Gathering here and there
A bud—the richest and rarest—
For a place in their long, dark hair.

Feeble and garrulous old men
Tell in the Spanish tongue
Of the good, grand times at the Mission,
And the hymns that the Fathers sung;

Of the oil and the wine, and the plenty,
And the dance in the twilight gray—
" Ah, these," and the head shakes sadly,
" Were good times in Monterey !"

Behind in the march of cities—
The last in the eager stride
Of villages later born—
She dreams by the ocean side.

The Monterey Whale Fishery.

The whale fishery, which for the last twenty-five years has constituted one of the most important of our local industries, is likely
soon to become a thing of the past.   The whales are gradually becoming scarcer, and now that the tide of commerce is turning this
way, they will, ere long, give our bay a wide berth.

Of the various species of whales which frequent the coast of California, the most valuable are the Sperm Whale, Right Whale,
Humpback, Finback, Sulphurbottom and California Gray.   Many
years ago, while California was yet a province of Mexico, the New
Bedford whale ships caught large numbers of Sperm and Right
whales along this coast; but these species have now almost disap-
peared, and our whalers have to content themselves with the more
numerous but less valuable California Greys and Humpbacks.
Occasionally, however, a Sulphurbottom or Right Whale is caught,
but this is a rare occurence.

It was for the purpose of catching the Humpbacks, known to be numerous in this bay, that the Monterey Whaling Company was organized in 1854. In the fall of that year, Capt. J. P. Davenport, an old and experienced whaler, got together a company of twelve men, only three or four of whom were regular whalemen, the balance being "land lubbers." They had two boats, and met with pretty good success, as the whales were tame and easily caught in the old fashioned manner with harpoons and lances. Capt. Davenport brought a number of bombs with him from the east, but owing to some defect, they proved worthless and were not used. The price of oil falling to twenty-five cents per gallon, the company was disbanded before the commencement of the next season.

The whales, however, were not allowed to rest, for in 1855 the company of Portuguese, known as the " Old Company," was organized with seventeen men and two boats. Although at first they used no guns, they succeeded in taking about 800 barrels of Humpback oil annually for about three years.

In the Autumn of 1858, Capt. Avery of the schooner *Sovereign* noticed a school of California Greys playing near the surf, about three miles from town. He informed the whalers of his discovery and they at once proceeded to the spot indicated and caught several of the school, besides many others of the same species, before the season closed. In the winter of the same year (1858) Capt. Davenport again started in with two boats well manned and equipped with bomb and harpoon guns. Both companies whaled in the bay with varying success, getting from 600 to 1000 barrels annually per company, for several years, when Capt. Davenport withdrew

5

from-the business.   His company has since been known as the
" New Company" of Portuguese whalers.   During the season of
1862–63 each company secured about 1700 barrels of oil.   This
was one of their most successful years.

In 1861 the Carmel Company was organized.   At first they
whaled in this bay, but in the spring of 1862 they moved to their
present station on Carmel Bay.

The Humpback season commences about the 10th of August
and expires about the first of December.   The California Grey
season then commences and continues until the middle of April.
The first half of the season is called the "going down season," as
the whales are then descending from their summer haunts in the
Arctic ocean to the lagoons and bays on the lower coast, for the
purpose of bringing forth their young.   It is during the "coming
up season," as their return northward is called, that the greater
number of whales are caught; for if the whalers can succeed in
striking the " calf" the "cow" is an easy capture, as she will die
rather than desert her offspring.

This brings us to the means of capturing these marine monsters.
At the first streak of dawn the whalers man their boats, six to a
boat, and proceed to the whaling "ground" near Point Pinos.
Here they lay on their oars and carefully scan the water for a
" spout."   Suddenly some one sees the wished-for column of mist
foam, and cries out " There she blows !"   Then all is activity, the
boat is headed for the whale and the guns are made ready to fire.
When within a short distance of the animal the oars are " peaked"
and the boat is propelled by paddles so as not to disturb the wary

whale. Having arrived within shooting distance, which is about forty yards, the harpoon, connected with a long line, is fired into whatever part of the animal is visible. Down goes the whale, the line with a turn around the " loggerhead " of the boat being allowed to run out for several hundred yards, when it is held fast. The whale generally makes a direct course for the open ocean, dragging the boat after with almost lightning rapidity. Soon, however, it becomes weary and comes to the surface to breathe ; now is the golden opportunity; the boat approaches as near as possible and a bomb-lance is fired. In case this enters a vital part, the animal dies instantly, but oftener it does not, and the same maneuvering as before is repeated until two or three bombs have been shot before the animal is killed. It is then towed to the try works, where the " blubber," as the casing of fat with which it is covered is called, is removed, cut into small pieces, and boiled out. Sometimes, however, the whale will sink as soon as killed ; should such be the case, a buoy is attached to the line, and the animal is left until the generation of gases in its body causes it to rise, which usually occurs in from three to nine days. It is then towed in and " tried out " as before.

The usual yield of a California Grey is about forty barrels if a female, and twenty-five barrels if a male. That of a Humpback about the same. The average size of a California Grey is forty-two feet in length, and twenty-eight or thirty feet in circumference. A Sulphurbottom is occasionally caught which measures a hundred feet from tip to tip. In 1873 the New Company commanded by Capt. Pray, captured a Right Whale seventy feet long and fifty feet in circumference.   It yielded 175 barrels of oil and 1500 pounds of bone, and netted the company over $2000.   At the close of that season the two companies, numbering in all thirty-four men, were consolidated into one company of twenty-three men, eleven quitting the business entirely.

The life of a whaler is very exciting and dangerous, as the boat is sometimes capsized or swamped, and the men have to swim for their lives.   Yet such is the force of habit, that they seem to feel no more fear when in pursuit of a whale than if they were upon dry land.

A good story is told of a gentleman who upon assuring the whalers that he knew not what fear meant, was allowed to go out with them in their boat.   Soon a whale spouted near by, and the Captain, true to his aim, lodged a harpoon in its body.   The whale made for the mouth of the bay, the boat almost flying in its wake. The amateur whaler now began to get excited, not to say scared. His teeth chattered, he prayed, and hung on to the boat like grim death.   Faster and faster went the boat, the water just even with the gunwale, and whiter and whiter grew the gentleman's face.   At length the limit of his endurance was reached.   He jumped to his feet and yelled out in frantic accents: "Cut the rope!   For heaven's sake cut the rope, I'll pay for the whale!"   The rope was not cut and the whale was secured without much difficulty.   All who wish to know more of this most interesting division of the cetaceans are referred to Capt. C. M. Scammon's excellent work, "Marine Mammals of the Pacific Coast."

Our Chinese Colony.

Chinatown is distant from Monterey about one mile from the outskirts of the town, and is situated on one of the numerous small bays that line the bay of Monterey. It is admirably selected for the business carried on by its enterprising citizens—fish-curing and abelone shell shipping. Its inhabitants are frugal, industrious, and well behaved. Little or no crime occurs among them, and so far as our experience goes, they are a sober, honest set of men, and compare very favorably with their countrymen throughout the State. "Tim," a California-born Chinaman, speaks English and Spanish as fluently as a native. The census of Chinatown is as follows: Man Lee Company, three men and three women; Sun Sing Lee Company, three men, two wonen, and three children; Yek Lee Company, six men, two women, and one child; Yee Lee Company, six men, two women, and three children; Man Sing Company, four men and one woman. In connection with these companies are those of Carmel, Pescadero, and Portuguese Bay—Sun Choy Lee Company, eleven men and one woman; Boo Lee Company, eight men, and Dai Lee Company, eight men. There are about twenty men and eight women outside of these companies in different employments in the town and neighborhood.

The Chinese industries are fishing for rockfish, cod, halibut, flounders, red and blue fish, yellow tail, mackerel, sardines, and shell fish, the greater part of which are split open, salted, and dried in the sun

5*

for exportation to San Francisco, whence they find their way to the mines throughout the State, and abroad. It may be estimated that the amount of dried fish exported from Monterey annually averages nearly 100 tons. The Chinese collect also large quantities of abelone shells, which find a ready market at $20 a ton. They possess about thirty boats, nearly all of which were built by themselves. They are sailed in the Chinese fashion. During the past month they have commenced shipping fresh fish to Gilroy, San José, and other interior towns. Although they import from San Francisco the greater portion of their merchandise, they purchase very liberally of the merchants in town, and as their trade is always for cash, they are very desirable customers in these hard times.

Pacific Grove Retreat—The M. E. Encampment Grounds.

The eastern boundary is about one-half mile west of Chinatown, and, following the sea-shore, the tract extends to the line fence of the dairy farm this side of the Light House. This last boundary is marked by a conspicuous pile of rocks, which, looking as if it might be a Druidical monument, is the termination of a promontory that breaks the force of the northwesters, and shelters the sea line of the tract. Under the lee of the promontory is a beautiful little cove, possessing a smooth beach, and being almost entirely free from surf. This is the spot selected for bathing houses. Behind this cove are pine woods, interspersed with oaks, covering a surface of sufficient extent and smoothness for the accommodation of any congregation of auditors. Here, therefore, as this survey indicates, will be placed the stand for the preachers. The site selected for the hotel, or hotels, occupies ground centrally located with reference to the sea, upon which the buildings, therefore, will look out directly. A broad avenue traverses the grounds, with side streets, separating lots, upon which villas are expected to be erected.

The general arrangements of the Encampment are based upon the principles guiding those of the Eastern States, especially the one held at Ocean Grove, in the vicinity of Long Branch, N. J., and are under the control of the Board of Trustees.

One hundred acres are divided into residential lots, a park, a pleasure ground, a grand avenue, minor streets and avenues, and the town. The lots are divided into sections, ranging from 30x60 to 30x125.

The principal buildings are the preachers' stand—an elegant structure, carefully and substantially built by Prinz, of Monterey, containing a platform for the ministers, and seats for the choir. It faces the congregational ground, which is arranged in a perfect circle, 200 feet in diameter, with a ring of tents around it, and a roadway of seventy-five feet. The aisles range from four to twelve feet in width. Benches are provided to accomodate about 5000 people. The whole is covered by the shade of the pines—tall, straight, young trees—through whose gothic branches the sunlight falls subdued.

The restaurant is a commodious building 33x90 feet, placed but a short distance from the congregational ground. It will be run on the ticket system, by R. C. Wormes. In close proximity are the grocery and provision store, 24x50 feet; the meat market is 24x50 feet, and the furnishing and clothing store.

On the opposite side of the street are six dormitories, each 24x50 feet. There is also a laundry.

Admirable arrangements are made for conveniences necessary to civilization.

The stable accomodations are a few rods off, on the Monterey side, around a large well.

The water for the use of the camp, in addition to three wells on the grounds, is brought 3300 feet in pipes from a tank containing 6000 gallons, filled from a never-failing stream, and is raised sixty-two feet above the level of the grounds; it flows into another tank, with a capacity of 15,000 gallons, having a clear fall to the highest point on the grounds, of twenty feet. Both tanks will be kept constantly filled, as a large quantity will be consumed in sprinkling the roads and grounds. There are also some very valuable sulphur and chalybeate springs within a short distance, which can be introduced without much trouble.

New tents can be bought on the grounds at wholesale prices, or rented at very low figures.

Ordinary campers, except during the meeting, will be charged fifty cents a head, to include wood, water, and cleaning up.

The bath-house is 60x24 feet, and contains twenty-two dressing rooms. It is conveniently placed in a small ravine on the verge of a beautiful little bay, whose sandy floor rivals in whiteness the marble of the Romans' bath. The water is transparently clear, and is always warm, being sheltered from the wind by picturesque rocky cliffs. The view of the numerous baylets and jutting rocks, over which the blue waves dash in merry sport, and the Gabilan Range in the foreground, is lovely in the extreme.

The Executive Committee are the Rev. J. O. Ash, of Salinas, the indefatigable Chairman ; the Rev. J. W. Ross, Geo. Clifford, Jas. Allayton, of San Jose; and Geo. F. Baker. Too much praise cannot be awarded to the resident managers, the Revs. Ash and Ross, for the pains and labor they have bestowed upon the arrangements, carefully considering even the most minute details in order that nothing should mar that perfect harmony so necessary to insure success ; nor should the liberality and untiring energy of Mr. Jacks be unnoticed, for by the aid of this gentleman's purse and advice many apparently insurmountable difficulties have been surmounted.

The Encampment commands a splendid view of the Bay of Monterey, and the magnificent scenery surrounding it, with pretty bays for bathing places and beautiful groves for rambles. In close proximity to the Light House ; within a morning's walk of that pearl of beauties, Cypress Point ; with good sea fishing, sailing, or boating ; with the opportunities for every kind of outdoor occupation and enjoyment ; and all within three miles of Monterey, and its railroad and steamboat connections with all parts of the State ;

with a climate beyond reproach; a temperature, with one or two exceptions, the most equable in the known world, and with a location so healthy that doctors scarcely make a living, it bids fair to become an unrivaled summer resort. Bishop Peck, now making an Episcopal visit on this coast, says : " I have some acquaintance with our splendid retreats for camp meetings and health in the East, and I have no hesitation in saying that this is fully equal to the best I have seen."

Point Pinos Light House

Is situated on an eminence and point of land forming the extreme western shore of the bay of Monterey, and distant from the town about three miles. The building is a dark gray stone structure, one and a half stories high, built in the strongest and most substantial manner. Rising from the center or ridge of the roof is a brick tower painted white, on which is firmly placed the iron lantern and illuminating apparatus, the exterior of which is painted red. This light station was erected by order of the Hon. Thomas Corwin, Secretary of the Treasury, in the year 1853. The light was first exhibited to mariners on January 20th, 1855, and Mr. Charles Layton was the first keeper appointed to take charge of it. The light is classed as a third order Fresnel, with catadioptric lenses, of immense and powerful magnifying capacity. The light, in ordinary fair and clear weather, should be discernable from a vessel's deck sixteen and one-half nautical miles. The height of center of focal plane above high water on sea level is 91 feet. The arc illuminated is four-fifths of the entire horizon, or 288 degrees. The description of the light, as given to mariners in their charts, is a third order, fixed white, Fresnel light.

The following persons have been principal keepers of the light: Chas. Layton, Charlotte Layton, Geo. C. Harris, Frank Porter, Andrew Wasson, and Capt. Allen L. Luce, the present attentive and courteous incumbent, who has held the position from October 1st, 1871.

The drive to the Light House is pleasant and pretty, and well shaded. The road passes the grounds of the M. E. Encampment. The view from the tower well repays the visitor for his pains. Capt. Luce and his family are always pleased to welcome visitors and to show them every attention.

MONTEREY.

BY MRS. ANNIE E. MERRITT.

Where the blue waves kiss the sand,
As they leap a joyous band;
Where the mountains towering high,
Seem to touch the azure sky;

Where the young vines meekly twine
Round the tall, majestic pine ;
Half enclosed in rocks of gray,
Gently slumbers Monterey.

Beautiful as poet's dream,
When its hills with verdure teem ;
When the balmy air is filled
With incense from heaven distilled,
And sweet Nature seeks repose
Where the murmuring streamlet flows,
Like some gem of brightest ray
There enthroned is Monterey.

Flowers of the brightest hue,
Laden with the morning dew ;
Velvet grass and clinging vine,
Groves of oak, and stately pine,
Fleecy clouds that lightly rest
On the evening's gentle breast ;
All these hold their quiet sway
On the shores of Monterey.

But more beautiful at eve'n
In the mystic light of heaven,
When the moon's pale, silvery sheen
Lends its beauty to the scene,

And a holy calm o'er all
Settles lightly as a pall,
And the night seems changed to day
'Neath the skies of Monterey.

Talk not of the storied Rhine,
Nor Italia's sunny clime,
Nor the Orient's so fair
With its balmy, perfumed air.
Crowned with old historic lore
Well I love this rock-bound shore ;
'T is to thee I sing my lay—
Queen of Beauty, Monterey.

Monterey as a Port.

We copy the following from the *Salinas City Index:*
" It requires no great stretch of the imagination to predict that the products of a very large area of California, both to the south and east of Monterey and Salinas, are ultimately to find their way to tide-water across our Valley.   In truth, between San Francisco and San Pedro, a distance of over four hundred miles, WE HOLD THE GATEWAY to the only accessible harbor for general commerce with

6

the world. It is only a question of time in regard to the centering of other railroads to this point. To the doubting ones we say, examine the profile maps of the country, then scan any map of the Atlantic seaboard, and answer us, whether in the light of what has come to pass elsewhere, we are extravagant in our predictions for the future.

" We would not give a fig for the judgment of that man who is despondent over our future prospects. There were just such in San Francisco twenty years ago, and with about as much reason and judgment as those who are fearful there is no further room for progress here."

The Monterey *Weekly Herald* says:

" Only a few years have elapsed since the first ship loaded grain at San Francisco for Europe; and when we compare the great fleet of vessels engaged in transporting our cereals to foreign ports with the number that were so engaged a few years ago, is it any wonder that the Californian's heart swells with pride, and that he dreams of how this great fleet shall be multiplied until it shall astonish the world?

" It is well, while the Californian is conjuring up such a brilliant future for his State, that he should pause in his reverie and ask himself what should be done for the proper protection of such vessels. It is well known that, during the prevalence of rough weather outside, a vessel cannot enter the harbor of San Francisco, and any arriving at such a time must of necessity put to sea, or come to Monterey, where nature has modeled a PORT OF REFUGE, with no 'bar' to guard its entrance, and free from all dangerous shoals and rocks. The storm of last Fall bears out this assertion, for the Bay was filled with all vessels within reach seeking refuge there, entering and leaving just as they pleased.

"But nature has not made our harbor so good that the hand of man cannot improve it; and we believe it to be the duty of those interested in the future welfare of our State, to properly represent to Congress the great good that would result from the expenditure of a small sum of money, compared to the benefits that would accrue to the shipping interests of this coast, in improving the port of Monterey.

"The harbor, properly, is in the shape of a horse-shoe, the mouth opening to the north, and it is amply protected from the south, east, and west; and with a breakwater extending half a mile into the Bay from the northwestern shore, the harbor would afford PERFECT SAFETY FROM WINDS FROM ANY AND ALL POINTS OF THE COMPASS. Even now the largest ships in the navies of the world can ride with safety through any gale that blows in the Bay of Monterey; but no doubt improvements can be made.

"There is also a large natural laguna, which could be without difficulty transformed into a dry or wet dock. In fact, the natural position of Monterey is such that she is bound to become, next to San Francisco, the most flourishing port on the coast. Her growth may be retarded, but it cannot be prevented."

The Monterey and Salinas Valley Railroad.

Whatever may be the fate of this road in the future, it will always be memorable in the commercial history of California as the first narrow-gauge railroad built in the State; and also as a road built by the people for the people, to contend with a great and powerful monopoly, and to save the grain-growers of the district no less than $200,000 a year.

It was commenced in April, and finished in October, 1874. All interested in it devoted their time and means without stint, especially C. S. Abbott, the President; D. Jacks, the Treasurer; and John Markley, the Secretary. Mr. J. F. Kidder, now engaged on the Nevada narrow-gauge, was the Chief Engineer and Superintendent of Construction. The iron came from the Pacific Rolling Mills of San Francisco, and Falkner, Bell & Co.'s, of the same place. The locomotives, " C. S. Abbott," and " Monterey," from the Baldwin Locomotive Co., in Pennsylvania. The cars, which are superior in every respect, were built in Monterey, by Thomas Carter.

Although the road is a " narrow-gauge," only three feet between the rails, the cars are so designed that the passengers hardly realize any difference from those of the broad-gauge, and have ample room and accommodation.

The railroad commenced running October 28th, 1874, too late to carry much of the grain of the Valley; but its early completion had been a fixed fact in August, thereby compelling the S.P.R.R. to make a reduction from $5.50 per ton to $4.25 freight on grain to San Francisco. The M. & S.V.R.R. carried about 6000 tons in 1874; loaded the H. L. Richardson at Monterey (2400 long tons). The freight on merchandise from San Francisco to Salinas City was $7.20; the S.P.R.R. reduced to $6.00. Salinas was supplied with redwood lumber from Watsonville and pine from San Francisco; now there are two markets open, and redwood is brought from Santa Cruz, and pine from Puget Sound, which comes to Monterey as cheap as to San Francisco, and only has to be freighted 20 instead of 120 miles.

The number of stockholders is 72, principally land owners or farmers, as may be seen by the following:

David Jacks has in Monterey Co. about...30,000 acres.
C. S. Abbott ....10,000 "
A. & M. Gonzales...................13,000 "
Robert McKee and Monrass Family, about..19,000 "
A. Wason .... 1,000 "
Francis Doud .... 1,000 "
P. Zabala......................... 5,000 "
Jesse D. Carr.....................45,000 "
James Bardin .... 5,000 "
John Abbott....................... 400 "
J. B. H. Cooper................... 5,000 "
C. Laird.......................... 2,000 "
Chas. McFadden.................... 500 "
6*

Malarin . . . . 5,000 acres.
Geo. Pomeroy 1,000   "
Judson Parson.   300   "
Wm. Quintal. . . . .   300' "
Wm. Robson   400   "
J. M. Soto. 3,500   "
B. V. Sargent 13,000   "
F. S. Spring. 2,000   "
Chas. Underwood   400   "
William Ford.   300   "

Besides the land owned and occupied by quite a number of small farmers.

The road, warehouses, wharves, cars, engines, etc., everything included, cost $357,000.

As regards the current year's freight: it costs by S. P. R. R. from Salinas City to San Francisco, freight $3.50, weighing and loading 25 cents, making $3.75 from Salinas to S. F. for all grain that is not stored in a warehouse; warehouse charges per season, $1.00 per ton. Weighing, loading, freight, and wharfage from Salinas to San Francisco, by Monterey and S. P. R. R., and G. N. P. Steamers, is $3.75 ; by M. & S. V. R. R. to Monterey is $1.75. In other words, it costs $3.75 to get the grain (when not stored) to deep water shipping, by S. P. R. R. to San Francisco, and $1.75 to deep water shipping at Monterey; if the grain is stored for the season, $1.00 per season.

Climate.

Monterey County has one of the most delightful climates in the world—neither too hot nor too cold. People here wear the same clothing winter and summer, there being so little range of temperature. THE TOWN OF MONTEREY HAS LESS RANGE OF TEMPERATURE THAN ANY PLACE ON THE COAST. The tables given below are prepared from the records kept at Salinas City, and are perfectly reliable in every particular. The following table speaks for itself on the subject of temperature, and is taken from the daily record kept by Dr. E. K. Abbott, who is a regular correspondent of the United States Signal Service :

MONTH, 1874.	Lowest temperature for month.	Highest temperature for month.	Mean temperature for month.
January..............	30 degrees.	66 degrees.	49 degrees.
February............	32 "	66 "	49 "
March...............	31 "	70 "	49 "
April...............	43 "	70 "	55 "
May................	45 "	82 "	57 "
June...............	53 "	79 "	59 "
July...............	52 "	75 "	62 "
August.............	52 "	76 "	61 "
September..........	47 "	76 "	59 "
October............	46 "	79 "	58 "
November..........	33 "	75 "	53 "
December..........	24 "	73 "	46 "

Observations of the thermometer were taken three times daily in the shade and open air. The lowest temperatures all occurred in the morning and were noted at 7 o'clock A. M., while the highest were noted at 2 P. M.. Our lowest temperatures are simply frosty nights, and are never continued during the day; for instance, our coldest night for 1874 is registered at 24 degrees; at 9 o'clock P. M. of the previous day the temperature was 34 degrees; while at 2 o'clock P. M. the same day the thermometer registered 62 degrees.

There was not a day during the entire winter of 1874–75 that a person could not gather a nice bouquet, grown in open air, from any of the flower yards in Salinas or Monterey. Fuchsias and geraniums grow all winter in the open gardens.

The following table shows the mean temperature of January and July in various portions of California and other States and countries, taken from reliable sources. Observe how little difference there is between January and July at Salinas City and Monterey:

PLACE.	January.	July.	Difference.	Latitude.
	Deg.	Deg.	Deg.	Deg.Min.
MONTEREY........................	52	58	6	36.36
Salinas City—1873.................	51	60	9	36.36
Salinas City—1874.................	49	62	13	36.36
San Francisco.....................	49	57	8	37.48
Los Angeles......................	52	75	23	34.04
Santa Barbara....................	54	71	17	34.24
San Diego.......................	51	72	21	32.41
Sacramento......................	45	73	28	38.34
Stockton........................	49	72	23	37.56
Sonoma.........................	45	66	21	38.18
St. Helena......................	42	77	35	38.30
Vallejo.........................	48	67	19	38.05
Fort Yuma......................	56	92	36	32.43
Cincinnati......................	30	74	44	39.06
New York.......................	31	77	46	40.37
New Orleans....................	55	82	27	29.57
Naples.........................	46	76	30	40.52
Jerusalem......................	47	77	30	31.47
Honolulu.......................	71	78	7	21.16
Mexico.........................	52	65	13	19.26
Funchal........................	60	70	10	32.38
London.........................	37	62	25	51.29
Dijon..........................	33	70	37	47.25
Bordeaux.......................	41	73	32	44.50
Mentone........................	40	73	33	43.71
Marseilles......................	43	75	32	43.17
Genoa..........................	46	77	31	44.24
Algiers.........................	52	75	23	36.47

—["Resources of Monterey County."

The following table of comparisons we extract from *The Natural Wealth of California,* by Titus Fey Cronise, a work which
though very valuable in its general information and research, is
extremely inaccurate in many points relating to Monterey.

Localities.	Spring	Summer	Autumn	Winter	Mean Tem. of the year
	deg.	deg.	deg.	deg.	deg.
San Francisco......................	56 5	60 0	59 0	51 0	56 6
Sacramento	56 0	69 5	61 0	46 5	58 0
Benicia............................	56 5	67 0	60 5	49 0	58 0
Monterey*.........................	54 0	59 0	57 0	61 0	55 5
San Diego.........................	60 0	71 0	64 5	52 5	62 0
Fort Yuma.........................	72 0	90 0	75 5	57 0	73 5
Humboldt Bay*.....................	52 0	57 5	53 0	43 5	51 5
Port Orford........................	52 0	60 0	55 0	47 5	53 5
Dalles, Oregon.....................	53 0	70 5	52 0	35 5	53 0
Astoria, Oregon....................	51 0	61 5	54 0	42 5	52 0
Fort Steilacoom, W. T..............	49 0	63 0	51 5	39 5	51 0

*The figures for these localities are probably too low.

METEOROLOGY.

The following is an abstract of meteorological phenomena observed by the late Dr. C. A. Canfield, at the city of Monterey, from October 1, 1863, to September 17, 1864.

Latitude 36 Degrees 36 Minutes, Longitude 121 Degrees 52 Minutes.

	Sept.	Oct. 1863.	Nov.	Dec.	Jan. 1864.	Feb.	Mar.	April.	May.	June.	July.	Aug.	Sept.
Greatest heat at 2 P. M.	......	83	77	66	73	74	74	84	76	76	71	77	72
Greatest cold 7 A. M. to 9 P. M.	45	40	33	40	39	44	41	50	52	53	55	51	......
Average heat at 2 P. M.	......	69	61	58½	60	63½	60½	65	65	65½	68½	68½	65½
Nights of frost	......	......	7	7	5	......	1	......	......	......	8	......	......
Rain in inches and hundredths	......	2 00	67	3 65	4	1 58	1 23	1 36	6	......	......	......	......
Days without clouds	4	5	1	2	9	3	6	......	1	3	6	1	4
Days completely clouded	1	0	3	3	0	3	0	......	4	15	19	1	1
South or southwest winds	9	7	8	5	4	15	14	27	8	6	3	10	......
North or northwest winds	17	15	14	21	15	12	16	9	13	7	9	2	......
Foggy mornings	6	3	9	4	6	2	7	7	8	14	11	2	......
Foggy evenings	5	3	4	4	5	3	4	5	7	8	3	8	......
Fog all day	1	......	1	2	......	......	1	3	1	8	3	2	......

Extract from Agricultural Report of 1869, by the late Dr. Canfield.

	January.	February.	March.	April.	May.	June.	July.	August.	September	October.	November.	December.
Maximum Tem..	63	71	71	68	80	83	80	80	94	90	77	65
Minimum Tem...	32	32	40	23	44	46	50	45	44	42	35	27
Mean Tem.......	50 3	49 4	56 1	43 1	58 9	62 8	65 7	61 8	62 9	59 5	55 1	48 9
Rain.............	3 83	4 13	2 69	....	1 09	0 03	0 01	....	0 02	1 36	0 72	2 42

The following remarks, among a multitude of others, we extract from the different well known journals to which they are credited ; being the unsolicited opinions of strangers who have visited Monterey at all seasons of the year, they are entitled to consideration :

THE CLIMATE IS REMARKABLY EVEN

And much milder than any place north of here ; oppressively warm days are unknown, and it is hardly ever unpleasantly cold.

For bathing purposes the beach is unequalled ; the slant is so gradual, and the tide ebbs and flows so lazily, the water is so delightfully warm and beautifully transparent, that a good.bath accommodation would attract thousands every summer. Such an establishment would pay handsomely here.

The strong south and southwest winds which detract so much from Santa Cruz on account of the unpleasantly cold weather they ofttimes produce, and so frequently cause the surf to become even dangerous for purposes of bathing, amount to but gentle zephyrs here.

I can assert from experience as well as from the testimony of many others, that it is the sleepiest spot in the State and the best place in California for the tired brain to rest.   *   *   *   * Men and women can sleep all night and all day, and grow fat and rugged and strong.   It is a real sleepy hollow, the only one in California, so far as known ; and this eminent quality, whether it be in the air or earth or sea or surroundings, it matters not, will be a fortune to Monterey if properly managed.

All who labor long and heavily with the brain must in their vocations have sleep, and they will frequent that place most where they can sleep best.

THE CLIMATE IS ALL THAT MAN CAN DESIRE.

Sheltered by the high pine-covered mountains on the west from the breezes of the ocean, the finely tempered wind odorous with the resinous pines and sweet scented shrubs comes gently stealing over the placid waters of the bay.   *   *   *   while the sea fog lifted high above by the hills scuds towards the great Salinas plain, fructifying the land and casting a thin cooling veil across the face of the sun.—*Sacramento Bee.*

7

THERE IS NO SPOT ON THE COAST

Whose natural advantages are at all equal to Monterey. Santa
Cruz is no comparison nor Santa Barbara either ; but these places
have the start, and only Yankee energy can bring Monterey up
with them. *   *   *   The first thing needed is a good hotel,
not in the town, but near to the woods and sea bathing. *   *   *
There are many great and wealthy men in Monterey who could, if
they would, build such a one as is required ; but they are natives,
and do not care for active life or investments of such a character ;
they are easy, slow-going people, content to let what they deem
well enough alone, and take no ventures of that character.—*Sacramento Bee.*

   For many years no town in the State has been less known than
Monterey. *   *   *   A quaint old Spanish town, without
life or movement, and apparently belonging to some forgotten arcadi-
an age. Yet for eighty years it was the most important town
in California, the seat of government and the commercial center.
*   *   *   The location of the old town is delightful—a gentle
grassy slope at the foot of the hills, of a moderate elevation, covered with evergreen trees and facing one of the finest harbors in
the world.

THE CLIMATE IS THE MOST DELIGHTFUL

That can be imagined. The only natural cause that brings life to
a close there is old age.—*Kern County Courier.*

MONTEREY IN A SANITARY POINT

Of view has been long known to stand second to no place in the world—no town of its size can show so many aged people who have spent all or the greater part of their lives at any one point, and no place where people hold age better.—*Salinas City Index.*

There is not one of the natural resources so much needed to make a successful and enjoyable watering place but can be found here.

A HEALTHY AND DELICIOUS CLIMATE,

Beautiful scenery, admirable facilities for bathing, sailing, riding, driving or hunting, with points of interest and beauty in the immediate neighborhood.—*San Francisco Daily Alta California.*

The Increase.

Within the past year twenty-five new residences and stores have been built in Monterey, and others are going up. Sixty new business enterprises have been started, twelve of them have collapsed, and several have removed to other portions of the town from which they settled in. These may be regarded as very substantial improvements, considering the unfavorable circumstances of the winter and the hard dry season. More than one hundred families have located at this place and in this vicinity during the same period.

That the trade of Monterey is steadily increasing in spite of the unfavorable season, is shown by the fact that the express business has increased nearly six fold since the opening of the railroad ; that fifty new business enterprises can make at least a living for their proprietors, while the business of their older rivals has not deteriorated ; that buildings of a substantial character are slowly but steadily increasing in number. Even the item of fresh fish and game shipments to the San Francisco markets through the express is of importance, since it embraces 90,000 pounds of fish, 8500 pounds of quail, 3500 pounds of deer and 3000 pounds of rabbits since the opening of the road.

Monterey Township Officers.

Town Trustees, S. B. Gordon, President, H. Escolle, Treasurer, W. H. Bryan, Clerk ; S. Pardee, W. H. Bryan, Justices of the Peace ; A. W. Rapelye, Matias Vargus, Constables ; W. D. Robinson, Road Master ; School Trustees—S. B. Gordon, B. V. Sargent, W. H. Bryan.

Monterey Post Office, Alvarado Street.

Post Office Hours.—Mail closes at 8 A. M.; arrives at 5 P. M.

Office hours—7 A. M. to 7 :30 P. M. on week days, and 8 to 10 :30 A. M. and from 4 to 7 P. M. on Sundays.

EXPRESS OFFICE, corner Pearl and Alvarado streets.—Mail closes at 8 A. M.; arrives at 5 P. M. Office hours—6 A. M. to 8 :30 P. M. on week days, and 7 A. M. to 12 and 6 P. M. to 8 P. M. on Sundays.

Church Services.

CATHOLIC CHURCH.—Rev. A. Casanova; morning, 10 A. M., Evening 3 P. M..

METHODIST EPISCOPAL.—Rev T. B. Hopkins, in Central Building. Morning, 10 :30 ; evening 6.

EPISCOPAL CHURCH.—Rev. J. S. McGowan, Washington Hall. 7 :30 P. M.

PACIFIC GROVE RETREAT.—10 A. M., 3 P. M., and 7 P. M.

NEWSPAPER, *Weekly Herald.* Every Saturday. S. Clevenger, Alvarado street.

Travel.

MONTEREY AND SALINAS VALLEY RAIL ROAD.

WEEK DAYS.—Leave Monterey 8 :30 ; arrive at Salinas 9 :45. Leave Salinas 3 :15 ; arrive at Monterey 4:30.

7*

SUNDAYS—Leave Monterey 8 A. M. and 4 P. M.; leave Salinas 9 :45 A. M. and 5 :45 P. M.

STEAMERS.

G. N. & P.'s steamers and opposition steamer, *San Vicente*, leave as advertised at the Railroad depot, Express and Postoffice.

Objects of Historical Interest in the Town.

The Cuartel on California street is a two-story, ruinous looking adobe building, with a balcony running around it. It was built in 1840 by J. Abrego, acting under orders from Alvarado, and cost $11,000, redwood then selling at $50 per 1000 feet, and nails at $36 a keg. The books of the Library Society are there, but for the present the Library is closed to the public. The Methodist Episcopal Church and Sunday School hold their meetings in the building. Col. B. C. Whiting is the agent for the government property in Monterey. The Cuartel was also used as the school house until the school was transferred to the

COLTON HALL.

This building stands back off Main street. Since the removal of the county seat to Salinas it has been occupied by the school. Prior to that time it was used as the court house; and for the county

offices.   We extract the following in regard to it from the Rev. Walter Colton's very interesting work, *Three Years in California :*
" 184——, March 8th.—The Town Hall, on which I have been at work for more than a year, is at last finished.   It is built of a white stone, quarried from a neighboring hill, and which easily takes the shape you desire.   The lower apartments are for schools ; the hall over them—seventy feet by thirty—is for public assemblies. The front is ornamented with a portico, which you enter from the hall.   It is not an edifice that would attract any attention among public buildings in the United States ; but in California it is without a rival.   It has been erected out of the slender proceeds of town lots, the labor of the convicts, taxes on liquor shops, and fines on gamblers.   The scheme was regarded with incredulity by many ; but the building is finished, and the citizens have assembled in it, and christened it after .my name, which will go down to posterity with the odor of gamblers, convicts, and tipplers."

THE PRISON

was first built by Walter Colton adjoining the old calaboose, but in 1855 a new and more substantial one was erected as the county jail, in the school house building.

Should Monterey ever recover her position as the county seat, it would be a great saving to the county, as there need be but little extra cost incurred for buildings.

THE OLD BLOCK HOUSE AND FORT

stand on the hillside overlooking the bay.   A weird adobe naturally attracts the attention to the spot. The view from the fort well repays the exertion of the walk. About the year 1843 Gen. Micheltorena dug a deep ditch on the site of the present fort, with two or three embrasures for guns which were never mounted. When the United States squadron under Commodore Sloat took possession of Monterey in July, 1846, the block house was built and ship guns mounted. It was first called Fort Stockton, but afterwards Fort Mervine. On the arrival of Co. F, U. S. 3rd Art., in January, 1847, earthworks were thrown up, and it was picketed and guns were mounted. It was dismantled in 1852, most of the guns being carried to Benicia. A few may still be seen at the corners of some of the streets.

THE OLD CUSTOM HOUSE.

" Pioneer," writing to the Monterey *Republican*, says : " The foundation, or rather the central portion of it, was laid when the flag of Old Spain waved over California, and after laying for years in that state, the walls were raised under Mexican rule, and a tiled roof put upon the central part. At the end were built two small towers, shingled over ; but the second tower was not built until 1844 or 1845. In the Mexican time the Custom House could boast of a boat and boat's crew, but now Uncle Sam is too poor to support one in the third harbor of California, though it is the only port where a vessel can lay in safety during southeasters, from San Francisco to San Diego. In early days it used to support two or three Custom House officers, for Monterey was the port where the duties were paid by the vessels trading to the Mexican Department or Territory of California. In the latter part of 1844 the Custom House, or central part of it, was turned into a ball-room by the officers of the U. S. Frigate *Savannah,* then laying at anchor in the bay of Monterey. * * * On the taking of Monterey by the U. S. Naval forces July 6th, 1846, the old Custom House was occupied by a party of marines, and the headquarters of Capt. W. Mervine of the U. S. Navy, who had command of the forces, was in the north end of the building."

The learned Dr. Canfield was for some time Collector of Custom at this port. He was succeeded by Mr. Ireland. Now, the port is, so far as the Customs are concerned, amalagmated with Santa Cruz and Moss Landing.

The building is occupied as a private residence by Capt. T. G. Lambert. It is charmingly situated at the end of Alvarado street, and seawards almost hangs over the bay. In the summer evenings the seats under the portico are occupied by young men and maidens, enjoying the balmy breezes, and sentimentalizing upon the moonlit wavelets as they break in ripples on the beach. It would be an admirable site for a small hotel.

THE CATHOLIC CHURCH.

Was built in 1794. It was within the Presidio enclosure, and was intended merely as a chapel for the accommodation of those who were unable to attend the parish church at Carmel. When the missions were secularized, the Carmel mission was abandoned and the Monterey chapel dedicated as the parish church. The material used in its construction was a kind of white stone, abundant in the neighborhood. Although this stone is quite soft, being easily cut with a knife, it has withstood the ravages of time remarkably well, and the building may stand for another hundred years. In shape, it was originally a parallelogram, 120 feet long by 30 feet wide, inside dimensions. In 1858, under the direction of Padre Juan Bautista Cormillas, two wings were added, furnishing increased capacity, and transforming the church into the shape of a cross. The altar was built at the same time. It is the work of an Italian, and is justly regarded as a fine piece of art. The large gothic windows are adorned with life-size paintings of various saints. The walls are also hung with paintings, many of them being of great age and exquisite beauty. They were principally brought from the mission of Carmel, and are by unknown artists. The church will accommodate five hundred people. It is by far the most interesting building in the town, and is an honor to the church it represents. The visitor who devotes an hour to examining this sacred edifice will be well repaid for his time. The present pastor is Rev. A. Cassanova, to whom we are indebted for much valuable information.

THE CEMETERY.

The Cemetery is situated across the slough or estero, near the Catholic church, and is connected with the town by a causeway of white stone. In shape it is an irregular triangle, surrounded on two sides by water, and on the third by a fence which is sadly in need of repairs.

Passing through the dilapidated portal, we find ourselves in the midst of a lovely growth of live oaks. Old and moss-covered patriarchs of the forest, which doubtless were standing long ere the Genoese stepped upon the eastern verge of the Continent, are grouped around in picturesque confusion. Trees of a younger growth, perchance acorns when beheld by Serra, are intermingled with these ; while the northern half of the Cemetery is overrun by a dense growth of lupins, covered with flowers of a most brilliant yellow. As these flowers, typical of jealousy, bloom for a short season above the ground, then fade away and merge into unremembered dust, so it is with the petty jealousies of this life about which we fret so much.

Near the center of the present inclosure are the remains of a stone wall that formerly marked the boundaries of the Cemetery as laid out by the old Franciscan Fathers. They inclose a space about one hundred yards square, and show that the Fathers must have believed in cremation, or else overrated the healthfulness of Monterey.

Upon the side nearest the bay are the trenches which surrounded a primitive fort erected by Governor Micheltorena, previous to the American occupation.

The graves are scattered here and there, with no regard to order —some beneath the shade of the giant oaks, others on the open grassy plats bathed in perpetual sunshine—in fact, wherever the friends of the departed deemed most appropriate. This very lack of order forms one of the characteristic beauties of the place. Were everything arranged with mathematical precision, the picturesque charm of the place would be lost.

After reclining for a while upon the fragrant grass, listening to the mournful dirge wailed by the wind through the trees, and the answering moan of the ocean—that grand symbol of eternity—we reverently retrace our steps and are soon once more in the land of the living, where too often the Grim Messenger is unthought of until his terrible knocking is heard at the gate.

CALIFORNIA'S FIRST THEATER

Stands on Pacific Avenue, and is an adobe building, the property of Mr. John A. Swan, one of our earliest pioneers, and a gentleman possessed of a great fund of information about the earlier days of the State. From the Monterey *Weekly Herald* and the Santa Cruz *Sentinel*, we extract the following information in reference to the first Thespian performances in the Golden State. "It was in the fall of 1847, that four volunteers, (Matt Gormley, Bill Tindal, Jack Moran, and Long Lee) came up from Santa Barbara on military duty, consigned to Co. F, 3d Regt. U. S. Artillery. They were in the minstrel line, and had given two burnt cork entertainments to the Santa Barbarians, before leaving. In Monterey they were joined by Aleck Patterson, Pete Earl, and three local characters designated as "Tips," "Taps," and "Tops." With this company, the "management" gave two performances in the old Cuartel Building, south end, up stairs. This was undoubtedly the first effort at minstrelsy on this Coast."

"The first theatrical performance ever given in California took place in the old adobe store-house adjacent to Jack Swan's saloon, and it came to pass in this way. About the time that Stevenson's regiment, New York Volunteers were disbanded, three companies including the Colonel came up to Monterey. Soon after, the soldiers attempted a theatrical exhibition, which was a success. Encoura ed by their liberal patronage, the managers induced Jack to fix seats, stage and scenery in the old adobe. The bills were got out in due form, posters printed with a blacking-pot and brush, and programmes written announcing ' *Putnam*,' or ' *The Lion Son of* '76,' as the first piece to be played. C. E. Bingham personated the '76 Son, and Mrs. Bingham Mrs. Martha Washington, Charley Cluchester George Washington. Frank Wensell and his wife took part. John O'Neal, Mr. Fury and Pete Earl belonged to the company also. *Damon and Pythias, Box and Cox, The Golden Farmer, Grand Father White Head*, and *Nan the Good for Nothing*, were pieces in the repertory of the company. John Harris, Tom Beech, Capt. Wingfield, Mrs. *Kettlebottom*, and Lieut. Derby, were also among the leading spirits of the troup. 1849 and 1850 were memorable eras in the Thespian records of Monterey."

THE CONVENT.

Another ruined, broken-windowed building on Main Street. It was built in 1852, for the Sisters of Charity, and used by them till 1858. The Monks resided in two small houses on the hillside.

8

THE OLD CALABOOSE

Was built in 1832, by Figueroa, and stood where Watson's butcher shop, and Sunoneau's saloon are now, at the junction of Pearl and California Streets.

THE OLD COMMISSARIAT

Was the building now occupied by E. H. Schmidt's store, on California Street.

Our Pioneer Residents.

Though death, and the other changes that time brings with his wings have sadly thinned the ranks of our pioneers, we still have a few left who have remained loyal to their first love, Monterey.

D. Jose Abrego, James Meadows, Thomas Bralee, Geo. C. Harris, George Oliver, John A. Swan ("Pioneer,") Wm. D. Robinson, George Austin, Teodoro Gonzalez, Manrico Gonzalez, B. V. Sargent, J. Flynn, then the youngest white boy in San Francisco, and D. Jacks, all of whom arrived in the State before, or in 1849.

Opinions of Disinterested Parties.

We extract the following from the speech of the Hon. P. A. Roach, last alcalde and first mayor of Monterey, and first senator from the County, at the centennial commemoration, on the 3d of June, 1870 :

" Look at this magnificent bay.   It stretches from point to point twenty-eight miles.   It can shelter the navies of the world.   Its anchorage is secure.   No pilot has ever been needed to bring vessels even to its wharf.   The largest ships ever constructed can ride at anchor within a few hundred yards of the beach.   The great seaports of the world are obliged to lay heavy charges on shipping for inward and outward pilotage.   The cost of this service in San Francisco for one year, or at the most, two years, would build in Monterey Bay a breakwater that would give *perfect security* in *all* weather ; but the United States Government ought to perform this duty.   Of late it has been seeking to obtain harbors in various sections of the world, which will require immense sums to place them in security.

" Why not devote some of the treasure to improve this harbor ? The ports of Monterey and Santa Cruz can soon be made great centers of shipment of merchandise.   A railroad could be constructed to bring, for shipment hence, immense quantities of grain from the San Joaquin region.   A railroad even within the county would bring produce to fill your grain elevators, and as in the past, Mon.

terey would become again in the markets of the world a place of commercial importance. Look at yonder *Estero*, bridged to lead from the Church to the Cemetery. There is a natural dock-yard by removing the sand bar that obstructs its mouth. It is deep enough to take in the largest ship, and was favorably reported on by many of the Naval Commanders. Why not adopted ? Because there was a combination on foot in 1849, of high speculators. Our people who owned land were made to believe that the convention, if called, would continue the Capital at Monterey; that the Barracks would be used, and that a naval depot would be established here. Then your people swapped lots in San Francisco for those in Monterey. You remember many of these bargains to your sorrow.

" Soon came the change ; the Capital was removed to San Jose ; then we saw the naval depot taken from us ; next we heard that wooden shanties were to be erected in the *healthier* climate of Benicia, for the army. These tinder boxes, and the expense entailed by the change, cost over a million dollars. I asked Governor Riley, the last military Governor of the Territory, why this change ? why abandon fire-proof quarters for the others ? The gallant soldier, and the honest, scar-marked veteran answered in his stammering manner, spec–spec–spec–speculation. That is what caused the quick blow against your city."

We extract the following from " Three Years in California," published in 1852.

" The scenery around Monterey, and the *locale* of the town, arrest the first glance of the stranger. The wild waving background of forest-feathered cliffs, the green slopes, and the glimmering walls of the white dwellings; and the dash of the billows on the sparkling sands of the bay, fix and charm the eye.' Nor does the enchantment fade by being familiarly approached; avenues of almost endless variety lead off through circling steeps, and winding through long shadowy ravines, loose themselves in the vine-clad recesses of the distant hills. It is no wonder that

CALIFORNIA CENTERED HER TASTE, PRIDE AND WEALTH HERE,

Till the vandal irruption of gold hunters broke into her peaceful domain. Now all eyes are turned to San Francisco, with her mud bottoms, her sand hills, and her chill winds, wnich cut the stranger like hail driven through the summer solstice. Avarice may erect its shanty there, but contentment and a love of the wild and beautiful will construct its tabernacle among the flowers, the waving shades and the fragrant airs of Monterey. * * * * *

The climate on the seaboard is REMARKABLY EQUABLE; it varies at Monterey, the year round, but little from sixty.''

Sea Bathing at Monterey.

The late Colbert A. Canfield, M. D., whose scientific researches have been of immense service to the country, writes as follows:

8*

" There is no better place on the coast, within easy access of the large towns of California, for a watering place, than Monterey. The climate, mild and salubrious; the beautiful natural scenery, landscapes and ' water-scapes,' with the wide, smooth bay in the foreground, all combine to make it the most attractive seaside retreat that can be found; for the Bay of Monterey is one of the most beautiful in the world. The town is sheltered from the cold northeast winds by the pine-covered hills on the side towards the ocean, and still its atmosphere is scarcely even hot or uncomfortably warm. It is, consequently, a very healthy place for all classes of persons, but especially for children. Hence it is, I suppose, that the children are as numerous in its streets as are the quails in its neighboring thickets. The summer complaints of children are almost unknown, and it is a long time since there has prevailed here any contagious epidemic disease. The water of the bay has one peculiarity, viz : it is much warmer than that of the ocean outside. There is a strong current running into the bay on the north side, around fort Año Nuevo, that makes a complete circuit of the bay, along the eastern shore, and running thence westward along the south shore by the town of Monterey, it runs out around Point Pinos, even against the wind, with so strong a current that it is very hard rowing against it in a boat. For this reason, the water near the town is several degrees warmer than it is on the Santa Cruz side of the bay. And also for this reason, I suppose, it is, that there is so much beautiful seaweed growing on the southeast side of the bay.

" Nowhere on the coast is there such a variety of beautiful and delicate forms of sea-weed, and such an abundance, as here. Collectors of the article for scientific or ornamental purposes are in their glory here, and many of the shells are not devoid of beauty or variety.

" The surrounding country contains much beautiful scenery, and interesting drives may be had in various directions * * * * with the certainty of a few hours of pleasant and healthful recreation. Within easy access of the town are plenty of opportunities for fishing or hunting, for those who like these sports."

Chalybeate Waters, or Iron Springs.

Dr. Canfield, having examined the springs at the Pescadero and Point Cypress, writes :

" The rocky cape that shelters the town of Monterey from the sea, and forms its harbor, is a ridge of granite, coarse and rotten, the most of it easily crumbling to pieces where exposed to the waves or air, and in many places colored red with the iron which it contains. As the surface water (from rains and fogs) passes through this porous granite, it dissolves out the iron, as may be seen in nearly all the springs that flow from this granite ridge towards the sea ; but only in a few places is the water sufficiently charged with iron to be · called chalybeate, and to be serviceable as a remedial agent.

" The springs containing a noticeable quantity of iron, are near the mouth of the Carmel river, in the ravines that have been cut through the sandstone rocks into the granite, running down to the sea. There may be seen here cropping out thin strata of iron ore (carbonate and hydrated oxyd) sometimes pure, and sometimes mixed with sand. This is a few rods south of the farm house at the Pescadero. One spring in particular, in a ravine near the sea shore, has its water so saturated with iron, that it is deposited in abundance around the margin of the pools, and on the sticks and stones in the water. There is no sulphur in the water, or next to none, and it is quite clear and palatable except for the iron which it contains. Here, then, we have a chalybeate water that will undoubtedly prove an excellent tonic for people who are debilitated and with but little blood in their veins, and it is also accompanied by all the other hygienic adjuvants necessary for the renovation of the strength of the feeble—a pure and healthy atmosphere, mild and warm—it being on the south side of the promontory of Point Pinos—cold bathing in the surf, as it rolls in from the ocean, or tepid baths in the warm and sheltered nooks among the rocks—as the state of the health requires, or fancy dictates. The surrounding scenery is beautiful. There are wide beaches with beautiful sands, shells and curiously water-worn rocks, with caves and natural bridges. The little bay of Carmel, in front, is dotted with rocky islets covered with the nests of sea birds, and across the bay, Point Lobos rears up its granite walls and turrets, resounding with cries of seals and sea-lions that make it their habitation. The anlon (abelone) shells are very abundant here, and it is a favorite resort of the Chinese fishermen. Numbers of handsome agates are found on the beach, and a mine of silver and gold (?) was once opened at the water's edge. This vein contains silver, perhaps, but the metalliferous gangue or matrix being crystallized gypsum, (sulphate of lime) it would hardly be possible that it could contain gold."

Our Coal Mines.

The principal mines in the course of development are the "Monterey," B. V. Sargent, President; A. Manuel, Secretary; the "Mal Paso," J. W. Miller, President; A. H. Harris, Secretary. There are also the Consolidated Coal Mining Co., whose offices are in San Francisco: A. J. Griffiths, President; E. Hayden, Secretary: and several others of minor importance. It is quite probable that in a few months Monterey will ship away large quantities of coal, as the prospects are highly flattering.

Our Wild Flowers.

We cull the following from the *San Francisco Chronicle*, as it is so thoroughly applicable to our own hill-sides and cañons, teem ing as they are with beautiful flowers, rare and graceful ferns, and odorous flowering shrubs.

"Whosoever has seen a little of California will forgive us for loving our wild flowers. They are so many and so beautiful that we cannot withhold the expression of our admiration. We used to love, and we love yet, the modest, shy little violet that in the East was almost snow-born, and which timidly put forth its azure petals on the first touch of May. We loved it for associations broken up long ago. But how little is the whole sisterhood of flowers at the East compared with the glories of a California Spring? We go out upon our hill-sides at that season and find miracles of beauty everywhere under our feet—not single flowers, but a wilderness of sweetness and beauty, never to be forgotten. We have counted in one morning twenty-nine varieties within less than the area of an acre, and some of them exquisitely pure in color and in symmetry. In all the foothills and mountain-sides of California, even far into its arid Summers, flowers burst up from among rocks which seem hardly able to give a foothold for aught so delicate and fragile, challenging your admiration, and almost seeming to rejoice that the wandering feet of a stranger have led him where his eyes could feast upon their beauties, which else had never been seen by man. Our gardens are beautiful with the chosen flowers of every clime and country, but the retiring beauties of our hill-sides and cañons have a charm for us that no tricks of the gardener's skill can imitate or approach."

MONTEREY TRADES DIRECTORY.

Hotels.

Washington, Lockwood & Bryan, Washington street.
Monterey House, Paulson & Lagoni, Alvarado street.
Bay View House, Private Lodging House, Main street.
Boarding House and Restaurant, M. Silvas, Pearl street.
Furnished Rooms, J. Simoneau, Pearl street.
Restaurant, R. C. Wornes, Tyler street.
J. Simoneau's Restaurant, Pearl street.

Dry Goods, Groceries, Cigars, and General Merchandise.

Wm. Bardin, Alvarado street.
H. Escolle & Co., California and Polk streets.
W. Laporte, Alvarado street.
L. Little, Washington street.
J. Abrego, Pearl street.
B. Mendessolle, Washington street.

Groceries and Provisions.

J. B. Snively, Alvarado and Pearl streets. Wells, Fargo & Co.'s
Agent.

E. H. Schmidt, California street.
F. Gomez, Alvarado street, Post Office.
M. Silvas, Pearl street.
W. H. Pyburn, Alvarado street.

Dry Goods.

L. Bergstein, Polk street.
S. Marks, Alvarado street.

Watchmakers, Jewelers, Gunsmiths, and Hardware Dealers.

McClure Bros., Washington street.

Silversmith, Engraver, and Draughtsman.

John Hall, Abrego street.

Silversmiths and Abelone Jewelers.

Celestino Truxillo, Alvarado street.
P. H. Masters, Alvarado street.

Tinsmith and Hardware Dealer.

W. W. James, Pearl street.

Vegetables, Fruits, Tobaccos, Stationery, and Notions.

L. B. Austin, Alvarado street.
Porter Long, Pearl street.

Butchers.

F. Doud, Alvarado street.
Thos. Watson, Pearl street.

Bakers.

Mrs. Bradwick, American Bread, Washington street.
H. Escolle, French Bakery, California street.

Lumber Merchants.

Lambert Bros., the Old Wharf, Railroad Depot.

Carpenters and Builders.

L. Boswell, Polk street.
G. Oliver, Larkin street.
H. Prinz.
E. J. Lewis, Alvarado street.
A. Guillée, Polk street.
G. Sullivan, California street.
C. Herron, Washington street.
J. Gray, Pacific Grove.
F. Graham, Pacific Grove.

House, Sign, and Carriage Painters.

St. Clair, Roberts & Trascol, Houston street.

Saddler and Harness Maker.

J. Cramer, Pearl street.

Boot and Shoe Makers.

Chris. Gamber, Pearl street.
A. Chacon, Pearl street.

M. Vargas, Houston street.
Manuel Bojorges.

Barber.

S. Koffle, Pearl street.

Plasterers.

P. Corley & F. Folsom.

Pianos and Organs.

E. E. Curtis, Main street.

Blacksmiths and Wheelwrights.

Dodge & Sanchez, Alvarado street.
A. B. Reed, Alvarado street.
A. Toothacher.

Saloons.

Wise & Harris, Pearl street.
J. Simoneau, Pearl street.

The Shades, R. Morey, Alvarado street.

The Union, D. Ruiz, Pearl street.

Railroad Exchange, A. Sanchez, Alvarado street.

Depot Saloon, J. Feraud.

Monterey Saloon, M. Dutra.

Railroad House Bowling Alley and Saloon, P. Serrano, Alvarado street.

Monterey Brewery, V. Gigling, California street.

Livery Stables.

Bryan & Bonny, Washington street.

R. Morey, The Shades, Alvarado street.

Teamsters.

R. Morey, Alvarado street.

John Myers, Washington street.

J. Caldwell, Main street.

Laundry.

Go Tai, California street.

THE COUNTY IN GENERAL.

The following pages in reference to Monterey County we extract from the very accurate and valuable work compiled by Mr. A. W. Butler, the " Resources of Monterey County." The work will be sent, free of charge, to any one applying to Mr. Butler, or Mr. Winham, of Salinas City, California. All persons intending to visit or reside in California should read it.

Monterey County.

This county lies between parallels 35 degrees and 45 minutes and 37 degrees north latitude, and the central portion of the county is in longitude 121 degrees and 30 minutes west from Greenwich ; is bounded on the north by Santa Cruz County and Monterey Bay, on the east by the counties of San Benito, Fresno, and Tulare, on the south by San Luis Obispo County, and on the west by the Pacific Ocean ; has an area of 3,600 square miles, or 2,304,000 acres of land, and its northern boundary lies south from San Francisco about 90 miles by railroad. There is a great diversity of

9*

soil, climate, and productions, owing to the peculiar manner in which the county is divided by mountains, hills, and valleys. The territory may be regarded as divided naturally into four sections, viz :

The Santa Lucia Mountains,

Which extend from Monterey Bay on the north into San Luis Obispo County, where the range unites with the Coast Range, and from the Pacific Ocean—out of which they may be said to rise—to the Salinas Valley east—a distance of some eighteen miles. These mountains are in most places very rough and steep, especially in the central and western portions of the range, so much so that some parts of the country have not been explored. They attain in the rougher portions a height of 5,000 feet. In these mountains are many places where water is plentiful and the surface of the country such as to furnish a good home. The number of inhabitants that find places in the little valleys and cañons, and on the mountain sides of this range, is increasing rapidly every year. These mountain homes, sheltered from the winds, possessing a delightful climate, have peculiar advantages in the production of fruits. Grapes, figs, peaches, apricots, oranges, lemons and semi-tropical fruits flourish here.

Higher up on the mountains are many small stock ranches, where there is always plenty of feed. Wood is everywhere abundant, and persons living in this section have quite a trade in this article. There are several coal mines eight or ten miles south of

Monterey that promise well, though they have not yet any efficient means of transportation from the mines to market, but it is said that a railroad can be constructed without much difficulty to Monterey. Gold has been discovered in several places in this range, but not in paying quantities. These mountains contain immense deposits of limestone, from which the very best quality of lime can be produced; and as lime rock is not found very abundantly in the State, this county will doubtless build up an immense trade in that article. In this district are located the famous Tassajara and Pariso and other hot mineral springs. The land is mostly unsurveyed Government land. Game of all descriptions, from the quail to the grizzly bear, abounds. The scenery is unsurpassed in extent, grandeur, or beauty.

The Great Salinas Valley

Lies between the Gabilan mountains on the east and the Santa Lucia mountains on the west, and opens upon Monterey Bay at the north, from which it extends over one hundred miles south, with a width of from six to fifteen miles, and contains an area of about 1,000 square miles, or 640,000 acres of land. Through the valley runs the Salinas River, which has a quicksand bottom, and carries a large volume of water in the wet season, but a small quantity in the dry part of the year. The principal tributaries of the Salinas are the San Lorenzo and Estrayo from the east, and the Arroyo Seco, San Antonio, and Nacimiento from the west. The lands of the valley may be divided into three classes :

First—The heavy, rich bottom lands, good for the growth of anything.   This soil is mostly black adobe, and in many localities contains just enough sand to make it work easily, thereby making not only one of the richest soils in the world, but also one of the pleasantest and easiest worked.   These lands sometimes produce over one hundred bushels of barley to the acre, and one tract near Salinas City, containing six hundred acres, has produced of wheat an average of sixty-five bushels per acre.   The lands, commonly known here as " sediment lands," belonging to this class, (although comprising a small portion of it) do not stand a drouth as well as some of the other lands.   The average crop of wheat on these lands may be set down as about thirty-seven bushels per acre, and of barley about sixty-four bushels per acre.

Second—The table lands, good for almost anything, and especially for wheat and barley.   These lands stand dry weather or a short supply of rain better than any other in the valley.   The average yield of these lands is, of wheat about thirty bushels per acre, and of barley about fifty bushels per acre.

Third—The upland, good for the production of wheat, barley, oats, and rye.   These lands lie close along the base of the mountains in the lower part of the cañons and among the lower hills, and differ very much in quality in different localities, some being as good land as there is in the valley, while other tracts are not so good.   Some of this land is the very best fruit land in the State, and will produce oranges, limes, lemons, peaches, apricots, almonds, figs, and the other fruits common to this section.

There were cultivated in this valley in 1874 about eighty thousand acres in crops of all kinds; from this acreage there were exported thirty-two thousand tons of wheat and twelve thousand tons of barley. For other crops we have no data, but immense quantities of potatoes, beans, hay, and other crops were produced. The land in cultivation, in 1875, is about 110,000 acres. The price of wheat has ranged for the last three years so as to give an average price of about $1.57 per hundred delivered at the depot in Salinas City. Barley is now selling at $1.50 per hundred. The Salinas Valley, in point of fertility and diversity of soil, has no superior in the State, and when this is considered in connection with its mild and healthful climate, the amount of tillable land, and its proximity to the commercial center of the State, the great advantages possessed for transportation of produce, and the cheapness of freights compared with the more remote sections of the State, it has no equal. For every mile a farmer in California places himself from San Francisco he has to pay for it in two ways—first, by the amount of extra freight on what he buys; second, by the amount of extra freight deducted from the market price of what he has to sell.

The use of this valley, as agricultural land, has been confined to the past six years; prior to that time stock-raising was the occupation of the people, and the land was held in large tracts of from three thousand to forty-nine thousand acres, and as a consequence, this is a NEW COUNTY AND COUNTRY. As these large tracts of land are now being cut up and sold off, a splendid opportunity is offered to any one that wishes to secure a good home.

The Gabilan Mountains

Extend from the Pajaro River, at the northern boundary of the county, through the entire length of the county. From the Pajaro River, going south, the first eighteen miles of the range is a system of low mountains, covered almost everywhere with grass and an abundance of timber. This part of these mountains is now nearly entirely occupied. The next thirty miles of the range is composed of high, rough mountains, which extend as far south as the San Lorenzo. From the San Lorenzo to the southern boundary of the county, these mountains are low, rolling hills, forming the foot-hills of the Coast Range, and are about twenty or thirty miles in width. In this section are several beautiful little valleys, among which are Peach-Tree Valley, Cholamo Valley, Indian Valley, Long Valley, Priest Valley, and several others, nearly all of which possess a good soil. These valleys have a delightful climate, peculiarly adapted to the growth of semi-tropical fruits. The land is nearly all unsurveyed Government land, and at present is used chiefly in the stock business. The Gabilan Mountains, in their climate and adaptability, closely resemble the Santa Lucia. This range contains immense deposits of lime-stone, and quicksilver has been discovered.

The Pajaro Valley

Is located along the northern line of Monterey County, and extends across the Pajaro River into Santa Cruz County. This valley possesses one of the most productive soils in the State. The Pajaro River runs westerly through this valley, and finds an outlet in Monterey Bay. This section is separated from the Salinas Valley by a low range of hills that extend from the Gabilan Mountains to Monterey Bay. The climate is similar to that of the Salinas.

The Assessor's Books for 1874

Show that the property in the county is worth about $10,000,000. The total number of acres of land, aside from town lots, assessed, is 764,995 ; this land is valued at $5,733,512, or about $7.49 per acre, and the value of the improvements on this land is put at $423,737. The personal property is valued at $2,401,275. The rate of taxation for 1874 was $1.66 on the hundred dollars ; this, however, is much higher than our ordinary rates, and was so fixed in order to get the county out of debt, and in this object it succeeded.

The Population.

Although we have no very accurate source of information on this subject, the population of the county is about 9,000, and is increasing so rapidly that, with no elections of general interest to cause voters to register, there have been registered in this county since the last general election, 1,746 aditional voters.

Land Titles

In this county have long been settled, and there is hardly a case of doubtful land title in the county. The Government land is nearly all unsurveyed, and where occupied, is held by the right of possession.

Price of Land.

Farming lands in this county range in price from $3 to $150, per acre, owing to quality and location. Bottom lands in the Pajaro Valley are worth from $80 to $150 per acre, while the rolling and hill lands sell at from $15 to $40 per acre. The low hill lands interspersed with small valleys, between the Pajaro and Salinas Valley, vary in price from $6 to $25 per acre with improvements; of these lands there are about fifteen or twenty thousand acres. The table lands of the Salinas Valley sell at from $30 to $60 per acre, while some sell as low as $15. The heavy bottom lands range in price from $50 to $100 per acre, and in the immediate vicinity of Salinas City sell at $100 to $250 per acre, in small tracts of from one to twenty acres. The uplands are worth from $3 to $25 per acre, owing to quality and location.

There is a vast quantity of unsurveyed Government land in the
hilly and mountainous parts of the county, now held by the right of
possession ; and these tracts are frequently offered in the market
for low figures for the right of possession and the improvements.
This possession gives no fee to the land, but gives to the purchaser
the right to occupy until surveyed, and then the first right to buy
at Government prices.   To parties unacquainted with our lands
the prices given above may seem high, but when it is understood
that these lands are unsurpassed in productiveness, and need no
irrigation ; that in dry seasons they produce good crops when
other sections fail ; that in wet seasons our lands yield immensely ;
that the county has such good facilities for transportation of produce ; that we possess advantages for harvesting grain not found
in many localities ; that we have a climate that is delightful and
especially adapted to the comfort of the farmer ; that good society
and good schools are found almost everywhere within our borders ;
and that every farmer who bestows the proper care and labor in
seed-time upon his land is almost beyond doubt assured of a
bountiful harvest; we think the prices will be attributed to the
merit in the lands and their surroundings.   One man may do a
foolish thing, but many are not apt to invest in lands that are sell-
ing for more than they are worth, yet in this county during 1874
there was sold $300,000 worth of land to men who had been rent-
ing and farming the lands they bought, and most of them made
the purchase-money from land.

10

Rent of Farming Land

Is from $2.50 to $10 per acre. Many of the renters pay a part of the crop, say one-third or one-fourth. Of course, the $10 land is the very best, and the renter can afford to pay the price. Farmers in Monterey County, paying the prices for land and rent given above, on an average have done better in the last five years than have the farmers of any other county in the State.

The Health

Of the people of this county is as good as in any section of the State. We have no chills and fever, no epidemic diseases. We possess a climate that in itself does not produce disease of any kind, an atmosphere that brings no malaria. There is no night in the year but is cool enough to afford a good, refreshing sleep under a pair of blankets, and none so cold that a person could not sleep comfortably in the open air under the same cover.

Schools.

There are now organized about thirty-two school districts in this county, and in these districts schools are maintained for most of the time during the year. The wages paid to teachers are such as to command good talent. For instance, several districts situated in remote parts of the county have the good judgment to pay their teachers from $30 to $100 per month, and thereby they secure as good teachers as are found in the towns. In no district in the county are low wages paid. The State and county provide ample means to give every child a good English education if the parents of the districts but see that they get the worth of their money. With fifteen children between the ages of five and seventeen years a new district can be formed. California has a good school system, and it is generally well administered. There are no private schools of any note in the county.

Stock-raising

Is still a prominent interest in this county, especially in the mountainous and hilly portions, which are covered with sheep and cattle. Horses are raised for the markets by many of the farmers, and the better class of horses find a ready sale. Some persons have given attention to the raising of hogs, and the number shipped from the county every year is very large. The raising of hogs is very profitable in connection with farming, dairying, etc. No kind of stock requires feeding, except such as are kept up, as they find sufficient grazing the entire year.

Monterey County is one of the best sheep counties in the State, but persons need not come here with the expectation of finding a cheap class of land in tracts large enough to feed bands of sheep of

10,000 and over.   Our lands, as a general thing in valleys, are too valuable for sheep pastures, and in the hills it is difficult to find pasturage for large bands in one locality.

Angora Goats.

The Cashmere or Angora Goat business is of late attracting considerable attention among wide-awake business men, and is thoroughly establishing itself as one of the substantial industries of this State.   In this county the Santa Lucia and Gabilan mountains contain many thousand acres of Government land just suited to the grazing of goats.

Dairying

Receives much attention, and persons engaged in the business find it very profitable.   One dairy, four miles from Salinas City, belonging to C. S. Abbott, produced, in 1874, about two hundred thousand pounds of butter, which yielded $70,000.   This is the largest dairy, but many others are doing proportionally well. Butter and cheese always find a ready market.   There are many small dairies scattered through the hills of this county.   The climate is peculiarly adapted to this business—there is probably no better in the State.

Flax and Mustard

Are cultivated to considerable extent in the county.

Sugar Beets and Mangel-Wurzels

Are considerably cultivated by persons who have stock to feed and have only a small tract of land. The crop is a great success, both as to the immense amount of feed produced, and as to the convenience for use. The yield, with proper cultivation in good soil, is from seventy-five to one hundred and fifty tons per acre. The crop can be left growing all winter, and taken up as required for use, and when the ground is wanted for a new crop, what remains of the old crop can be pulled up and thrown into a pile. The mangel-wurzel grows to be very large, some of them grown around Salinas City weighing from ninety to one hundred and seventy pounds.

Potatoes

Are extensively cultivated, and make in many localities immense yields and are very profitable. Monterey County is one of the best potato counties in the State—both as to the quantity and quality of the crop.

10*

Alfalfa

Does well in almost every locality in this county, and produces from three to four crops of hay, of from two to four tons per acre every year, where it is used for making hay, and furnishes a perpetually green pasture, good for all kinds of stock, where used for the purposes of pasturage.

Pumpkins

Are also raised largely for feed on places where there is no outside range. One farmer in Pajaro produced one weighing two hundred and twelve pounds.

Beans

Are extensively cultivated in this county, the profit of the crop being large.

County Officers.

County Judge, W. M. R. Parker; Sheriff, J. B. Smith; County Clerk, John Markley; Recorder, Herbert Mills; Treasurer, B. T. Nixon; Assessor, W. V. McGarvey; School Superin-

tendent, R. C. McCrosky; Tax Collector, M. Castro; District Attorney, M. Farley; Auditor, J. B. Scott; Surveyor, F. L. Ripley.

BOARD OF SUPERVISORS.—E. St.. John, S. B. Gordon, J.
Sheehy, E. Breen, J. B. H. Cooper. Regular meetings, first Monday in February, May, August and November.

THE COURTS.—County Court, W. M. R. Parker, Judge; meets
on first Monday in March, May, July, September and November.
District Court, Belden, Judge; meets on the third Monday in
March, July and November. Probate Court, Parker, Judge; in
chambers at the Court House, in Salinas City, every Saturday, at
10 o'clock A. M.

Salinas City

Is the county seat of Monterey County. It is located on the
Southern Pacific Railroad, one hundred and eighteen miles from
San Francisco, ten miles from tide water at Moss Landing, and
eighteen miles by Monterey and Salinas Valley Railroad from the
harbor at Monterey. It is a young and thriving town, only seven
years old; and, situated as it is in the central portion of the rich
agricultural lands of the Salinas Valley, is one of the finest business
localities in the State. The population of the city has more than
doubled in the last two years, and is still increasing as rapidly as

ever. Enterprise and prosperity are everywhere visible. According to the annual report of the Mayor for last fiscal year there was spent for public improvement about $60,000. The city is well supplied with gas and water, and a well organized and equipped fire department. The school buildings are ample and commodious, and the schools of the town employ six teachers at present. There are eight church organizations presided over by pastors, viz: Methodist Episcopal Church, Methodist Episcopal Church South, Presbyterian Church, United Presbyterian Church, Episcopal Church, Christian Church, Baptist Church, and Catholic Church. Of Lodges, there are the Independent Order of Odd Fellows, Free and Accepted Masons, Independent Order of Red Men, the Patrons of Husbandry, and the Sons of Temperance. The rate of taxation for 1874–75 was forty cents on the $100 of property. The assessed value of property for 1875 is about $1,500,000. This is the great central point in Monterey County of trade, wealth, and commerce, and from its natural surroundings must of necessity continue to be so. It would be a good investment for persons acquainted with the business to establish woollen mills here, as this county produces large quantities of wool. The annual clip of the county is about seven hundred thousand pounds. San Benito, formerly a part of Monterey County, also produces large quantities of wool. A boot and shoe factory would do well here. An establishment for the manufacture of sugar from the beet would find this a good location. Machine shops and foundries of various kinds would find plenty of business here. We have but two flouring mills. Wagon and carriage factories would find a good field at this place. We need a good college here, as there is no institution of the kind in the county, and our climate is peculiarly adapted to the wants of pupils. Many of the manufactured articles that we have to buy might be procured at home. What we especially need is more capital, and we think that there is no place on the coast where a man that has money can go and do better than he can here; there are many good investments to be made.—[*Resources of Monterey County.*

SALINAS CITY DIRECTORY.

Mayor, H. S. Ball; Common Council, W. D. Reynolds, G. A Tolman, S. Cassiday, M. Hughes, C. Hoffman, S. P. Carter; City Marshal, W. W. Elliott; City Clerk, A. W. Butler; City Treasurer, S. W. Conklin; City Attorney, N. G. Wyatt; City Surveyor, St. John Cox; City Assessor, W. L. Carpenter.

EPISCOPAL CHURCH—Corner of Gabilan and California streets; Rev. J. S. McGowan, Rector; services every Sunday at 11 o'clock A. M.; Sunday School at 10 o'clock A. M.

CHRISTIAN CHURCH—Preaching every other Lord's Day at the Court House, by Elder Byram Lewis, at 11 o'clock, A. M. All are invited to attend.

UNITED PRESBYTERIAN CHURCH—Sabbath school and Bible class at 10 o'clock A. M.; services every Sabbath at 11 A. M. and 7 P. M., at Pacific Hall, in Salinas City. Prayer meetings every Tuesday evening alternately at the residences of the different

members.   Seats free.   All are cordially invited to attend.   Rev.
Geo. McCormick, Pastor.

M. E. CHURCH—Rev. Geo. O. Ash, Pastor; services in new
church on Gabilan street, at 11 o'clock A. M. and 7:30 o'clock P. M. ;
class meeting at 12 M. ; Sabbath school at 2:30 P. M. ; prayer
meeting every Thursday evening at 7:30.

M. E. CHURCH SOUTH—Preaching every Sunday at 11 o'clock
A. M., and 7:30 P. M. ; Sunday school at 10 o'clock ; prayer
meeting Wednesday evening at 7:30 o'clock.   Rev. Mr. Renfro,
Pastor.

PRESBYTERIAN CHURCH—Central Avenue ; Sabbath school at
9:45 o'clock A. M. ; Dr. W. H. Davies, Superintendent ; services
at 11 o'clock A. M. and 8:30 P. M.   Seats free.   All are cordially
invited to attend.   Rev. W. H. Wilson, Pastor.

SALINAS LODGE No. 204, F & A. M.—Stated meetings on
Saturday, on or before the full moon in each month.   Sojourning
brothers invited to attend.   W. V. McGarvey, W. M. ;   E. K.
Abbott, Secretary.

ALISAL LODGE No. 163, I. O. OF O. F.—Meets every Wednesday
evening at 7 o'clock, in Odd Fellows' Hall, Main Street, Salinas
City.   Members of the order in good standing invited to attend.
G. A. Tolman, N. G. ;   H. W. Mills, R. S. ;   Jas. McDougall, P. S.

IMPROVED ORDER OF RED MEN.—Gabilan Tribe, No. 44, meets
every Tuesday evening at Grangers' Hall.   Visiting and sojourning
brothers in good standing invited to attend.   A. Bullene, S. ;   L.
Auker, C. R.

PATRONS OF HUSBANDRY.—Until further notice, Salinas Grange

No. 24, Patrons of Husbandry, will meet at Grangers' Hall, over Vanderhurst, Sanborn & Co's store, on the 1st and 3d Saturdays of each month, at 2 o'clock P. M., for business.   J. R. Hebbron, Master; Wm. Quentill, Overseer; F. Johnson, Lecturer; Geo. Abbott, Chaplain; Peter Matthews, Steward; S. D. Triplett, Assistant Steward; Mrs. Killburn, Ceres; Mrs. Cony, Pomona; Mrs. Ida Hebbron, Flora; Mrs. P. Matthews, L. A. S; Clara Westlake, Secretary.

THE MAILS.—For Castroville, Watsonville, and all points north of Salinas City, mails close at 11 A. M.; for New Republic, Natividad, Monterey, and all points south of Salinas City, at 2:30 P. M.

POST OFFICE.—Closed on Sunday from 10:30 A. M. to 3 P. M.

Southern Pacific R. R. passenger train leaves Salinas depot going north 11:15 A. M., going south, 2:45 P. M.   M. & S. V. R. R. for Monterey, 3:15 P. M.   On Sundays, 9:45 A. M., 5:45 P. M. Excursion tickets good from Saturday night to Monday morning.

Salinas City Fire Department.—Chief Engineer, J. B. Langford; First Assistant, J. D. Brower; Second Assistant, R. L. Robbins; Secretary, L. H. Garrigus.   Engine Co. No. 1; Foreman, Jas. Swasey.   Alert Hook & Ladder Co. No. 1; Foreman, W. L. Carpenter.   Excelsior Hose Co. No. 1; Foreman, J. C. Kelly.

Castroville.

This thriving town was started in 1863, by Juan B. Castro, one of the owners of the Castro Grant.   Mr. Castro, through his skillful management and business energy, has succeeded in making Castroville, from a wayside station, a town of about 800 to 900 inhabitants.

The business establishments of this place are, two good hotels, two livery stables, five stores, one tin shop, one millinery shop, three saloons, one brewery, one flour mill, two blacksmith shops, one newspaper, post office, express, W. U. and A. & P. telegraph offices, drug store, tailor shop, shoe-maker, two churches and a fine school house.

Castroville being within three miles of the shipping point for much of the country back of it, and a great part of the traffic unavoidably passing through it, commands a large share of trade far up the valley, while in its immediate vicinity are the immense Moro Cojo, Bolsa Nueva, Santa Rita and Escarpinos ranches, containing some 39,000 acres of most excellent agricultural, grazing and wood land, which are being rapidly sold off in small farms, besides the Cooper and other large ranches that are rented to substantial tenants.

Castroville is a growing town, located on the Southern Pacific Railroad, two and one-half miles from Moss Landing, fifteen miles northwest of Monterey and nine miles north of Salinas City.   The trade of the town commands a good population. School facilities are excellent, and there are two churches in the place. The town is immediately surrounded by fine agricultural land, well watered, while to the east of Castroville, about three miles distant, there are large tracts of grazing and timbered land, a considerable area of table lands and rolling hills, the soil of these being sandy and well adapted to the raising of stock and the growing of fruits, vegetables, oats, rye, etc. Water is attainable in the town and vicinity at from six to fifteen feet. The average yield of adjacent lands is of wheat thirty bushels per acre, and of barley fifty bushels; one hundred bushels of barley per acre have been raised in some cases. The agricultural lands around Castroville are well suited to the growing, not only of wheat and barley, but to the successful cultivation of oats, corn, beets, potatoes and vegetables. The health of the town is exceptionally good, and the climate equable.— *Resources of Monterey County.*

Castroville Directory.

Wm. Childs, Justice of the Peace; J. W. Mitchell, Justice of the Peace; G. Alderman, Constable; P. Ojeda, Constable; Juan Pomber, Roadmaster.

11

POST OFFICE.

Mails close, going north, at 11 o'clock A. M.   Going south, at 2 P. M.   Israel Johnson, P. M.

SOUTHERN PACIFIC R. R.

PASSENGER TRAIN leaves Castroville Depot, going north, at 11:40 A. M.   Going south, at 2:25 P. M.

FREIGHT TRAIN leaves, going north, at 12 M.   Going south, at 5 P. M.

M. AND S. V. R. R.

Castroville Crossing.—To Salinas, 9:30 A. M.; Monterey, 3:30 P. M.   Sundays, to Salinas, 9 A. M. and 5 P. M.; Monterey, 10 A. M. and 6 P. M.

F. AND A. M.

CONFIDENCE LODGE, No. 203, F. & A. M.—Stated communications on the Saturday evening preceding each full moon, in Tolman's Hall, Castroville.   A. P. Potter, W. M.; L. Wollinberg, Secretary.

I. O. O. F.

CASTROVILLE ENCAMPMENT, No. 37, I. O. O. F.—Meets first and third Tuesdays of each month, at Odd Fellows' Hall, Castroville. J. M. Pomber, C. P.; M. M. Speegle, Scribe.

SALINAS LODGE, No. 163, I. O. O. F.—Meets every Saturday evening, in Odd Fellows' Hall, Castroville. M. M. Speegle, N. G.; F. L. Whitcher, R. S.

P. OF H.

MORNING STAR GRANGE, No. 188, P. of H.—Meets in Tolman's Hall, every two weeks, commencing April 3d, 1875. F. Brown, M.; Miss M. Paton, Sec.

CHURCH SERVICES.

Rev. O. D. Kelly, of Watsonville, will preach in the Union Church every Sunday at 3½ o'clock P. M. Sunday-school at 2½ P. M.

The Catholic Church, Rev. Father Kern, services at 10 o'clock A. M. on Sundays.

Newspaper—The *Argus*, published every Saturday.

.Moss Landing

Is located on the Bay of Monterey at the mouth of the Salinas river, about three miles from Castroville, and has three extensive and commodious warehouses for the storage of grain, and a substantial wharf running out into the bay about 1000 feet, where vessels lie to take in grain.   A regular line of steamers call twice a week.

Santa Rita

Is a small town situated about three miles from Salinas City.   The County Alms House, under the charge of Dr. S. M. Archer, is located here.   The town also boasts of a fine Catholic church.   Although situated too near Salinas City ever to become a large place, it must always remain a thriving little village.

Soledad

Is a thriving little town started in 1874, and is the present terminus of the Southern Pacific Railroad: Situated in the midst of a splendid agricultural country, perfectly level up to the fertile foothills, with crops that never fail, well watered by the river, and having water within twenty feet of the surface, it is bound to become a town of some importance. A fine school house is now being erected. The coast line of stages to the South connects with the Southern Pacific Railroad.

Chualar

Is a rising agricultural town on the Southern Pacific Railroad, situated in a beautiful valley, well watered, and with good lowlands and foothills. The climate and crops are equal to the best portions of the Salinas Valley. It is distant about ten miles southeast of Salinas, and will probably become a town of some importance.

Gonzales

Is another new town about twenty miles southeast of Salinas, in the heart of the Salinas Valley. With good lands, well watered, a good season would make town lots very valuable.

Natividad

Is a pretty little town at the foot of the Gabilan Range, about six miles northeast of Salinas City.

11*

The Mission of Soledad

Was founded October 9th, 1791, and is situated fifteen leagues southwest of Monterey on the left bank of the Salinas river, in a fertile plain known by the name of the " Llano del Rey." The priest was an indefatigable agriculturist. To obviate the summer drought, he constructed, through the labor of his Indians, an aqueduct extending 15 miles, by which he could water twenty thousand acres. In 1826 the mission owned about 36,000 head of cattle, and a greater number of horses and mares than any other mission in the country. So great was the reproduction of these animals that they were not only given away but also driven in bands into the bay of Monterey in order to preserve the pasturage for the cattle. It had about 70,000 sheep and 300 yoke of tame oxen. In 1819 the Major domo of this mission gathered 3400 bushels of wheat from 38 bushels sown. Its secularization has been followed by decay and ruin.— *Walter Colton.*

The mission possessed a fine orchard of a thousand trees, but very few were left in 1849. There was also a vineyard about six miles from the mission in a gorge of the mountains.

It is 18 miles from Monterey to Buena Vista, and 25 from there to Soledad : the road could be shortened by bridging some of the gulches. The road passes through some beautiful oak groves, affording perfect shelter from the sun and wind ; it is like traveling through a fine park. The left bank of the Salinas river should be followed, as it is superior in beautiful scenery and shelter from sun and wind to the right or main bank, and commands charming views of the Santa Lucia range, whose foothills are covered with mosaics of acres of flowers of the most brilliant hues, and of·gentle slopes covered with gnarled and curiously shaped oaks. From Soledad to San Antonio by the Relese cañon is 30 miles, or by the stage road about 45 miles; for campers and lovers of nature's beauties the horse trail through the cañon is by far the pleasantest, as there is an abundance of wood and water on the road, and finer and grander scenery for those who can enjoy it.

The Mission of San Antonio

Was founded by Padre Junipero Serra, July 14th, 1771, and is situated about twelve leagues south of Soledad on the border of an inland stream upon which it has conferred its name. The buildings were inclosed in a square, twelve hundred feet on each side, and walled with adobes. Its lands were forty-eight leagues in circumference, including seven farms, with a convenient house and chapel attached to each. The stream was conducted in paved trenches twenty miles for purposes of irrigation; large crops rewarded the husbandry of the Padres. In 1822 this mission owned 52,800 head of cattle, 1800 tame horses, 3000 mares, 500 yoke of working oxen, 600 mules, 48,000 sheep and 1000 swine. The climate here is cold in winter and intensely hot in summer. This mission on its secularization fell into the hands of an administrator who neglected its farms, drove off its cattle, and left its poor Indians to starve.—*Walter Colton's Three Years in California.*

The mission grapes were very sweet; wine and aguardiente were made from them in early days, and the grapes were brought to Monterey for sale. The vineyard and garden walls are now gone, and the cattle have destroyed the vines; many of the buildings are down, and the tiles have been removed to roof houses on some of the adjoining ranches. The church is still in good repair. There was formerly a good grist mill at the Mission, but that also, like the Mission, is a thing of the past.—*Pioneer M. S.*

Mission of San Juan Bautista.

This Mission looms over a rich valley ten leagues from Monterey —founded 1794. Its lands swept the broad interval and adjacent hills. In 1820 it owned 43,870 head of cattle, 1360 tame horses, 4870 mares, colts and fillies. It had seven sheep farms, containing 69,530 sheep; while the Indians attached to the Mission drove 321 yoke of working oxen. Its storehouse contained $75,000 in goods and $20,000 in specie. This mission was secularized in

1834; its cattle slaughtered for the hides and tallow, its sheep left to the wolves, its horses taken by the dandies, its Indians left to hunt acorns, while the wind sighs over the grave of its last Padre.— *Walter Colton.*

Hollister.

Hollister is the county seat of San Benito county; it contains a population of about 2000, and is one of the most thriving and prosperous towns of the State. It is pleasantly located in the center of one of the most beautiful and fertile valleys on the Pacific Coast.

It is situated on one branch of the Southern Pacific Railroad, of which it is the practical terminus—94 miles, or about five hours' ride from San Francisco. This road passes through the finest and most picturesque section of the State; the intermediate stations embracing the following prominent towns and cities, to wit: San Mateo, Belmont, Redwood City, Menlo Park, Mayfield, Mountain View, Santa Clara, San Jose and Gilroy. The celebrated Gilroy Mineral Springs, resorted to by invalids and visitors from all parts of the world, are about 20 miles distant, and the noted Paso Robles Springs of San Luis Obispo are located 180 miles southwest from Hollister.

Some of the most celebrated watering places of the coast can be reached by rail or vehicle in a few hours. Santa Cruz, known all over the world for its grand scenery and beautiful beaches, is 40 miles distant; and Aptos, a new rival as a pleasure-seeking resort, is nine miles this side. Watsonville, a cool, shady and delightful place to spend a few days of the hot season, has a nice beach five miles from town, reached by a fine gravelly road—is 23 miles from Hollister. Last, though not least, is the " CITY BY THE SEA"—the ancient capital of the State, Monterey, which is about 44 miles distant. Its natural charms and advantages as a watering place have been embalmed in song and told in story so often that we need not here descant upon them.—*Resources of San Benito County.*

San Juan Township.

The above township, in which is situated the old and once flourishing town of San Juan, adjoins Hollister Township on the west. It is delightfully located, and contains beside its beautiful and fertile lands, many objects of interest—not the least among which is the antiquated Mission of San Juan Bautista, with its tile roof.

San Juan Township lies in the northeast part of San Benito County, and contains an area of about 60,000 acres. The San Benito river passes through it near its northern boundary from east to west, and unites with the Pajaro river at the county line. There are about 9000 acres of rich bottom and valley land, about 4000 or 5000 acres of rolling land suitable to cultivation; the balance grazing land—some timber, but small, being used principally for fuel.

Fine flowing wells of pure water are obtained in the bottom lands at the depth of 100 feet; but good water can be had nearer the surface—say from 15 to 20 feet. The hill lands are well watered.

The Mission of San Juan Bautista was founded about the year 1775, and the church was built soon afterward, together with the adjoining buildings.

This place was once occupied as a military station, and was fortified during the Mexican Revolution in 1822. The location of the town is excellent, being situated on the bluff on the southwest side of the valley. It contains a population of about 500 inhabitants.

The nearest depot on the railroad is Sargent's Station, six miles; the next nearest is Hollister, nine miles. Stages run daily, carrying the mails each way.—*Resources of San Benito County.*

ERRATUM.

Page 15, after McDowell, read:

Although McDowell was the duly elected Mayor, he never served as such, the duties of the office being discharged by Mr. Charles Herron.

[128]

Monterey and Salinas Valley
RAILROAD.

Connecting at Salinas City with Southern Pacific Railroad for

San Francisco, San Jose, Soledad, Paso Robles Springs, and all Points East, North and South.

At Monterey, with G. N. & P.'s Passenger Steamships for

Santa Cruz, San Simeon, San Luis Obispo, Santa Barbara, Los Angeles, and all Points on the Coast South of San Francisco.

The most desirable route to *Santa Cruz, Aptos, Pescadero, and Soquel; Point Pinos, Moss Beach, Point Cypress, Old Carmel Mission, and Pacific Grove Retreat.*

No Staging, Four Steamers Weekly between Monterey and Santa Cruz.

JOHN MARKLEY,
Gen. Ticket Agent.

JOSEPH W. NESBITT,
Superintendent.

[1]

CHARLEY'S
RESTAURANT,
Oyster and Ice Cream Saloon,

TYLER STREET,   Back of Washington Hotel.

Meals at all hours. Ball Suppers and Dinners made a specialty. Board $5.00 a week and upwards. Fresh Eastern Oysters and Ice Cream always on hand.

PRIVATE ROOMS FOR FAMILIES.

Fresh Bread, Pies and Cakes every day. Three tickets for 25 cts.

R. C. WORNES, (late of Salinas City) Proprietor.

Families supplied with Fresh Eastern Oysters.

Orders by Mail Promptly Attended to.

LAMBERT & BRO.
—DEALERS IN—
Flooring, Fencing, Building Material,
And all kinds of Dressed and Rough Lumber,

Mouldings, Doors, Windows, Lath and Lime, Hair, etc.

ALVARADO STREET, MONTEREY, CAL.

Lumber Furnished by the Cargo.

Having supplied ourselves with a new improved Shingle Mill, we are prepared to supply shingles at a lower rate than can be done by others.

Lambert Bros. have purchased and thoroughly repaired the Old North Pacific Transportation Co's Wharf, at Monterey, and are prepared to do

Wharfage, Storage and Commission Business.

Agents for the opposition Steamer "SAN VICENTE," leaving Pacific Street Wharf, San Francisco, arriving at Monterey on *Friday Evenings.*

[8]

LINFORTH, KELLOGG & CO.
HARDWARE
And Agricultural Implements.

SOLE AGENTS FOR

PITTS' CHICAGO THRESHER,

MANSFIELD STEAM ENGINES,

WOOD'S EAGLE MOWERS,

RUSSELL'S PEERLESS MOWER and REAPER,

GARDEN CITY PLOWS,

MYER'S EXCELSIOR GANG PLOW,

NAPA GANG PLOW,

FRIEDEMAN HARROW,

FURST & BRADLEY'S SULKY RAKES,

TIFFIN HORSE RAKES,

GENEVA DO.

Full Supply FORKS, HOES, SHOVELS, RAKES,

AXES, HATCHETS, Etc.

Pumps, Hydraulic Rams, Rubber Hose, Belting, etc.

Church, School, and Farm Bells, Lawn Mowers.

Please send for Illustrated Catalogue and Price List.

3 & 5 Front St., San Francisco.

12   [129]

HALLET, DAVIS & CO.'S

Celebrated Pianos.

The Leading Instruments of the World!

Endorsed by

LISZT, STRAUSS, LEUTNER AND BENDEL !

GEO. WOOD & CO.'S

PARLOR and VESTRY ORGANS.

W. G. BADGER, Sole Agent, Nos. 7 and 13 Sansome St., S. F.

E. E. CURTIS, - - - - - - Agent for Monterey.

L. BOSWELL,

Contractor, Carpenter and House Builder

Has opened Shop in

ABREGO'S BUILDING,

And is prepared to take Contracts for

Building, Moving, Raising and all kinds of Carpentering.

[130]

[131]

FLOWERS,
FRUITS AND VEGETABLES.

D. H. LENOX'S

FRUIT AND VEGETABLE STORE,

Main Street, Salinas City,

Receives fresh supplies of Fruit and Vegetables from San Jose daily.

John C. Morrison, Jr.

Importer and Wholesale Dealer in

FINE WINES AND LIQUORS,

316 Sacramento Street,

And 321 Commercial Street, bet. Front and Battery,

SAN FRANCISCO.

MANUEL DUTRA'S
MONTEREY SALOON,
PEARL STREET, MONTEREY.

Best Brands Wines, Liquors and Cigars

G. M. WELLS, M. D.

Monterey City, - - - - - Cal.

Graduate of Medical College of Virginia, and Medical College N. Y.

Special attention given to Surgery and Diseases of Women.

DR. LEMON'S DENTAL ROOMS,

Up Stairs, in Ball & Frank's Building, Main Street,   SALINAS CITY.

Beautiful gold filling for $1.00 and upward, and warranted for life. Beautiful and substantial Sets of Artificial Teeth on any kind of base desired.
Terms moderate. All work freely guaranteed to give satisfaction.
I will be in Salinas from the 1st to the 15th of each month; after that time can be found at my Office in Monterey City. Calls by mail promptly attended to.   *G. B. LEMON, M. D., Dentist.*

J. SIMONEAU,
Lyon's Ale Depot, Monterey.

Bohemian Club Rendezvous.   The Best Liquors and Cigars.
FRENCH RESTAURANT.   MEALS AT ALL HOURS
Good Cheer and Good Reception.

FOR
Dry Goods, Clothing, Boots and Shoes, Hats and Caps, and all kinds of Furnishing Goods,
Go to S. MARKS.

He has just received a NEW STOCK, which he will sell cheap for Cash.

S. MARKS, Alvarado Street, Monterey.

12*   [133]

Washington Hotel.

LOCKWOOD & BRYAN, Proprietors.

This Commodious Three Story Hotel affords Superior Accommodations to the traveling public, being adapted to the comfort and convenience of

TOURISTS AND PLEASURE SEEKERS.

The Rooms are Large, Comfortable and Well-Furnished. The Table is supplied with

THE BEST THE MARKET AFFORDS.

Charges are very Moderate and suited to the times.

A good Ball Room is connected with the Hotel.

LOCKWOOD & BRYAN.

Homesteads for All!

DESIRABLE LOTS

IN THE RAPIDLY GROWING

TOWN OF CASTROVILLE,

For Sale at Moderate Prices!

Possessing varied advantages of beauty of location, convenience to business, fertility of soil, and all the requisites for a profitable, comfortable and beautiful Homestead. Size, 50 feet front by 130 feet depth. An alley 40 feet wide runs through each block. Most excellent water from 10 to 16 feet deep.

Sickness is almost unknown, so healthy is the town.

Being within three miles of the shipping point for much of the country back of it, and a great part of the traffic unavoidably passing through it, Castroville commands a large share of trade for up the valley, while in its immediate vicinity lie the immense Moro Cojo, Bolsa Nueva, Santa Rita and Escarpines Ranchos, containing some 39,000 acres of most excellent agricultural, grazing and wooded lands, which are being rapidly sold off in small farms; besides the famous Cooper, and other large ranchos that are rented.

The advantages above enumerated, and many others, will be apparent to any who will come and see for themselves.

JUAN B. CASTRO,

Castroville.

[137]

LAND FOR SALE!

2OO Acres of Land

FOR SALE,

On the Bolsa Nueva y Moro Cojo Rancho,

Distant 8 miles from Castroville, 8 miles from Salinas City, and 4 miles
from Santa Rita and Natividad.

The Land contains about

Two Thousand Cords of Wood,

Several Springs, and is suitable for Grazing, or the
Growing of Fruit and Vegetables.

For further particulars inquire of

J. D. CASTRO,

CASTROVILLE.

SEND FOR THE

RESOURCES

——OF——

MONTEREY COUNTY,

CALIFORNIA,

Including the Great Salinas Valley.

COMPILED BY A. W. BUTLER.

Published by the Mayor and Common Council of Salinas City, for FREE DISTRIBUTION.

M. & S. V. RAILROAD.

TIME TABLE.

Train No. 1.   A. M.

Leave Monterey................8 30
"   Bardin's.................9 15
"   Castroville Crossing......9 30
Arrive Salinas City............9 45

Train No. 2.   P. M.

Leave Salinas City.............3 15
"   Castroville Crossing......3 30
"   Bardin's.................3 45
Arrive Monterey................4 30

Sunday Excursion Trains.

Train No. 1.   A. M.

Leave Monterey................8 00
"   Bardin's.................8 45
"   Castroville Crossing 9 00
Arrive Salinas City............9 15

Train No. 2.   A. M.

Leave Salinas City............ 9 45
"   Castroville Crossing.....10 00
"   Bardin's 10 15
Arrive Monterey..............11 00

Train No. 3.   P. M.

Leave Monterey.... ....4 00
"   Bardin's.................4 45
"   Castroville Crossing......5 00
Arrive Salinas City............5 15

Train No. 4.   P. M.

Leave Salinas City ....:..5 45
"   Castroville Crossing......6 00
"   Bardin's.................6 15
Arrive Monterey..............7 00

Through tickets from San Francisco to Monterey and from Monterey to San Francisco, via the Southern Pacific Railroad, including omnibus transfer through Salinas City, for sale at S. P. R. R. Ticket Office, San Francisco, and the Company's Office in Monterey.

JOSEPH W. NESBITT,

Superintendent.

COUNTY DIRECTORY.

Courts.

DISTRICT COURT—Belden, Judge. Terms of Court—Third Monday in March, July and November.

COUNTY COURT—Parker, Judge. Terms (five)—First Monday in March, May, July, September and November.

PROBATE COURT—Parker, Judge. In perpetual session.

Board of Supervisors.

E. St. John,   S. B. Gordon,   J. Sheehy,   E. Breen.
J. B. H. Cooper.

Regular Meetings—First Monday in February, May, August and November.

County Officers.

Wm. M. R. Parker....................County Judge.
M. Farley.......................District Attorney.
J. B. Smith...............................Sheriff.
John Markley.......................County Clerk.
B. T. Nixon............................Treasurer.
H. N. Mills ....Recorder.
J. B. Scott..............................Auditor.
M. A. Castro.......................Tax Collector.
R. C. McCroskey...........School Superintendent.
Dr. H. P. Tuttle, Coroner, and ex-officio Public Administrator.

Newspapers.

Salinas City—" Index," " Democrat," " Town Talk."
Monterey—" Weekly Herald."
Castroville—" Argus."

[143]

A. ROMAN & CO.

Publishers, Importers, Booksellers and Stationers,

WHOLESALE AND RETAIL.

NO. 11 MONTGOMERY STREET,

LICK HOUSE BLOCK,   SAN FRANCISCO.

JOHN G. HODGE & CO.

Importers and Wholesale Stationers,

327, 329 and 331 Sansome St., cor. Sacramento,

New York Office, 59 John St.   SAN FRANCISCO.

Daniel Bigley.   Geo. Bigley.

BIGLEY BROTHERS,

Dealers in Groceries, Provisions, Etc.

N. E. Corner Clay and Davis Streets, San Francisco.

E. P. Fellows & Co.

Importers & Dealers in Druggists' Glassware & Sundries,

318 CLAY STREET, BELOW BATTERY,

P. O. Box, 1792.   SAN FRANCISCO.

Agents for Fritzche, Schimmel & Co's (Leipzig) Essential Oils and Flavoring Extracts.

Theo. Bagge.   Joseph Brook.   Chas. Jas. King.

C. JAS. KING OF WM. & CO.

Manufacturers of Hermetically Sealed Goods,

N. W. COR. BROADWAY AND SANSOME STREETS,

SAN FRANCISCO.

[144]

L. B. AUSTIN,

ALVARADO STREET, MONTEREY, Next to the Express Office,

CIGARS, TOBACCO, ETC.

Candies, Nuts, Etc., Stationery, Blank Books, Show-Case Goods, Vegetables and Fruits.

TASSAJARA SPRINGS now Open to VISITORS

The undersigned gives notice that the Tassajara Springs are now open for Visitors. These Springs were noted centuries ago among the old aborigines for the Medicinal Virtues of the waters, and the pale faces are now adding their praises to that of the red man to the Great Spirit for tho gift. Parties visiting the Springs can be furnished with meals, or, if camping, with provisions. Also, parties wishing to be taken to or from the Springs can be accommodated.   Apply to   **J. B. BORDEN.**

W. H. PYBURN,
Keeps a First-Class Stock of

Groceries and Provisions, Wines, Liquors, Tobaccos,
Fruits, Candies, Glass and Crockery Ware.

The W. U. Telegraph Office. Hides, Game and Farm Produce Shipped.

ALVARADO STREET.

Ornamental Trees at the Cypress Nursery.

Cypress Trees, Australian Gums, and Pine Trees in large quantities at Low Rates.

All orders promptly attended to by   -   -   **PAUL ROMIE, Monterey.**

DOMESTIC BAKERY.

MRS. BRADWICK,

Fresh American Bread, Cakes, Pies and Confectionery,

WASHINGTON STREET, NEXT TO THE HOTEL.

THE CONSOLIDATED TOBACCO COMPANY

OF CALIFORNIA.

PLANTATION AT SAN FELIPE. FACTORIES AT GILROY.

MANUFACTURE

CIGARS AND TOBACCOS

Of California Grown Leaf;

Cured by the Culp Process, and Guarantee them SUPERIOR
to anything Manufactured in the United States,

OF AMERICAN GROWN TOBACCOS.

Office and Salesroom, 207 Front St., San Francisco.

EDGAR BRIGGS, Agent.

SHADES SALOON.

MAIN STREET,

Near its Junction with Alvarado Street,   MONTEREY, CAL.

Choice Liquors, Wines, Cigars, etc.

Fine Billiard Table.

The Saloon is supplied with everything necessary to the comfort of visitors.
☞ Connected with the Saloon is a commodious

FEED AND BOARDING STABLE,

Where parties from a distance can be sure to have their horses properly attended
to.   ☞ Horses taken in charge for training.

R. MOREY, Proprietor.

THE NEW

CITY HALL.

Traveling Troupes desirous of performing in Monterey

· will find this Hall

Commodious, Convenient and Cheap.

For terms address the Secretary,

CITY HALL CO., Monterey, Cal.

[147]

[148]

[149]

STOVES and RANGES

---

[152]

DR. ABORN,

THE WELL-KNOWN SUCCESSFUL SPECIALIST,

Until he retires from active practice in a short time, will receive a limited number of patients daily, from 10:30 A. M. to 3 P. M., and from 6 to 7:30 P. M.

CONSUMPTION,

ASTHMA, BRONCHITIS, OZENA AND CATARRH,

DEAFNESS,

AND ALL DISEASES OF THE EYE AND EAR,

And Obstinate Chronic Diseases generally, embracing also

Heart, Liver, Stomach, Nervous Diseases & Broken-Down Constitutions

Are the class of maladies which are successfully treated by DR. ABORN,

CORNER OF POST AND KEARNY STREETS,

After the ordinary methods have failed.

RETIREMENT FROM ACTIVE PRACTICE.

DR. ABORN will retire in the course of a few months from active practice for a while.

MUTUALLY DESIRABLE.

It would be more agreeable to the Doctor if persons who desire to consult him would satisfy themselves as to his skill and successful mode of treatment before calling. This would tend to remove misapprehension and all necessity for explanations.

SEVERAL HUNDREDS

Of Testimonials from well-known citizens have been published in behalf of the suffering; also, a list of References, embracing some of our most prominent residents, whose names have been given so that the most skeptical may with all others have every opportunity of satisfying themselves that the peculiarly successful scientific method of treatment adopted by DR. ABORN is everything that it is represented to be. Evidences have accumulated in proof of this, grateful testimonials of remarkable cures being daily received by him. Many of these are contained in the pamphlets and papers published by him for gratuitous circulation.

ROUTES TO MONTEREY.

From San Francisco,

By Southern Pacific Railroad to Salinas City. Depot, corner Fourth and Townsend Streets. Train leaves at 8.30 A.M.

From Salinas City to Monterey, by M. & S. V. R. R. Train leaves Salinas at 3.15 P.M., on week days, and 9.45 A.M. and 5.45 P.M., on Sundays.

OR,

By Steamers leaving Washington Street Wharf every Tuesday and Saturday.

From Los Angeles, San Diego, and other Points South.

By Goodall, Nelson & Perkins' Steamers, sailing as advertised.

OR,

By Coast Line of Stages to Soledad ; thence by S. P. R. R. to Salinas City; thence by M. & S. V. R. R. to Monterey.

☞ Through Tickets for sale at S. P. R. R. Depot, cor. Fourth and Townsend ; and at Office of G. N. & P. S. S. Co., 238 Montgomery Street, San Francisco.

www.ingramcontent.com/pod-product-compliance
Lightning Source LLC
Chambersburg PA
CBHW020555270326
41927CB00006B/845